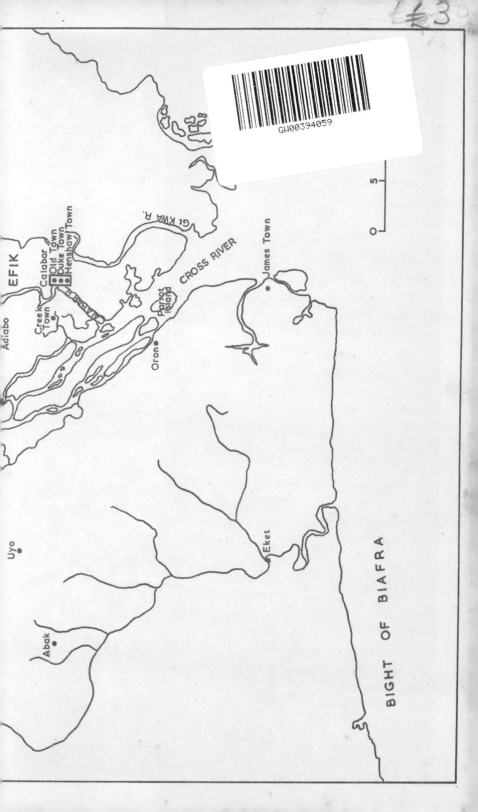

GOD AND ONE REDHEAD

Mary Slessor of Calabar

by

CAROL CHRISTIAN and **GLADYS PLUMMER**

I'm a witness to the perfect joy and satisfaction of a single life—with a tail of human tag-rag hanging on. It is rare— It is as exhilarating as an aeroplane or a dirigible or whatever they are that are always trying to get up and are always coming down!—Mary Slessor

HODDER AND STOUGHTON

Printed in Great Britain for Hodder and Stoughton Limited,
St. Paul's House, Warwick Lane, London, E.C.4., by
Ebenezer Baylis and Son, Limited, The Trinity Press,
Worcester, and London

FOREWORD

THE HANDPRINT OF the Christian missionary lies across Africa, its impress wide in span but open-fingered, varying as much in depth as in its tracings and textures. It may be seen as a pattern of life-giving irrigation, or as a scar across indigenous folkways, or even as an empty glove, a hollow deception.

Doctrines taken to Africa in the nineteenth century may alter unrecognisably in the twentieth, institutions may be destroyed, but remarkable individual missionaries are not forgotten. They worked, often, out of hearing of their own language, without news of their own countries, without, it would seem, anyone to recognise their value or spread their fame. Yet they made an astonishing impact.

Such a one was red-haired Mary Slessor, half saint, half hoyden. She was twenty-seven when, in 1876, she left her home in Dundee and the linen factories where she had worked since she was eleven, to join the Calabar Mission in West Africa. She can scarcely have known herself that she possessed qualities which were to make her a vital force in the life of that strange, awakening region and a heroine of heroines in her native Scotland.

Soon after her death the editor of the monthly *Record of the United Free Church of Scotland*, W. P. Livingstone, published his widely-read biography, *Mary Slessor of Calabar*. He followed it with an account specially written for children, *The White Queen of Okoyong*.

With these books was born a legend, the legend of the mill-girl who became a missionary, of the Great White Ma, of the White Queen. Pamphlets, articles, Sunday school books poured from the religious presses. In Scotland she was all but canonised. A memorial Room, in Dundee's City Museum has as its centrepiece a stained-glass window depicting the main episodes of her life. The apotheosis was complete when, in 1956, Queen Elizabeth laid a wreath at the foot of the cross above the grave of Mary Slessor on Mission Hill in Calabar.

All this would have humbled and amused her. Her reaction might well have been that of Shaw's Saint Joan: "But fancy me a saint!" Though she, too, could add: "I was always a rough one . . . But my head was in the skies; and the glory of God was upon me."

ACKNOWLEDGEMENTS

THE AUTHORS WISH to thank the Women's Foreign Mission of the Church of Scotland for permission to make use of the Livingstone biography of Mary Slessor, of which they hold the copyright, in the preparation of this book.

We express our gratitude to all those connected with the Church of Scotland Mission, both active and retired, who have generously offered suggestions, answered inquiries and provided anecdotes out of their own experience.

Thanks are due to the Rev. T. W. Jarvie of the Wishart Memorial Church, to Mr. W. S. Taylor and Mr. D. Torbet, City Librarians, and to Mr. J. D. Boyd, Curator of the City Museum, Dundee. Also to Mr. I. C. Cunningham of the National Library of Scotland, Edinburgh; to Miss Dorothy Holman, of the Museum, Topsham, Devon; and to Mr. H. G. Tremayne, pastor of the Topsham Congregational Church.

For personal reminiscences we are indebted to the following: Mr. Daniel MacArthur Slessor, who made extensive notes on the adopted children, the Rev. Nwachuku Eme, from whose own story we have quoted, and Professor Eyo Ita, all of Calabar; the late Miss Mina Amess, who worked with Mary Slessor; and the Rev. C. W. Wakeman and Mr. Daniel E. MacArthur, who remember her.

We are grateful to Miss Miriam Hattrick for information about Charles Morrison and his family; to Mr. H. R. Lingwood and Mr. John Partridge for sidelights on Charles Partridge; to Professor G. I. Jones for notes on the Okoyong people; and to Mr. T. G. Davies for help with map-making.

CONTENTS

ILLUSTRATIONS

Key to Acknowledgements
[1] By courtesy of the Central Library, Dundee
[2] Reprinted from *Nigeria Magazine*
[3] By courtesy of Daniel Slessor

INTRODUCTORY NOTE

SINCE THIS BOOK was begun, some of the place-names in it have become internationally synonymous with suffering. Calabar Province, where Mary Slessor worked, borders what has come to be known as Biafra. Ikot Ekpene, in particular, has been bitterly contested by opposing armies until, its farms destroyed and its people starving, it became a focal point for world-wide horror. Readers who have made the acquaintance of the people south-east of the Niger through the events of the Nigerian Civil War may want to know that it is certain of those tribes that are described in the following pages.

I

WILD LASSIE

IN THE MARGIN of one of her Bibles, against the verse of the Psalm that goes "I will not be afraid of ten thousands of people", Mary Slessor jotted the comment, "God and One are always a majority". It was a reflection of her mature years but a premise on which she had acted from early youth. While she was with God, she was of the major party—the odds were with her.

To the ordinary observer, however, the odds would appear to have been heavily stacked against the second of the seven Slessor children ever lifting herself out of the grim city streets of her childhood or of making much mark within them. Her father drank away the family earnings, leaving her gentle mother the mainstay of a family, all of whom were characterised as "delicate". Even before Mary, at eleven, began work in the textile mills of Dundee she was shouldering, as eldest daughter, most of the cares of the household.

She was born at Aberdeen on the 2nd December, 1848, year of ferment and revolutions, to Robert Slessor, a shoemaker, and his wife, Mary, a weaver. They made their first home at Gilcomston on the outskirts of Aberdeen.

Mary's birth took place in the home of Mrs. Slessor's mother in Mutton Brae, a steep, poor little street that echoed with the rattle of weavers' shuttles. Nearby, at Belmont Street United Presbyterian Church, she was christened Mary Mitchell Slessor, after her mother. And there, later on, she attended the Sunday school which began her education. The hard-worked children of the "hungry forties" were lucky if they received any other.

It was a grim period in Scotland, with the population turning from the uncertainties of agriculture to those of industry, which also proved to have its fat and lean years. In the towns there were almost no facilities for recreation. The churches, which offered help, hope and a glimpse of a wider world to the serious-minded, were also the agencies which banned playhouses as immoral and closed down parks and museums on Sunday—the only day of the week when the working populace might have enjoyed them. Yet the whisky shops were apparently unaffected. In one Scottish city at this time they outnumbered the bakers by more than six to one. The public houses, too, did a thriving trade.

Offered the choice—one emphatically could not have both—between God and Bacchus, kirk and tavern, Robert Slessor preferred the tavern. One wonders why. His wife's piety seems to have been generous and wise, at least where her high-spirited daughter was concerned, and not of a bigoted narrowness that would drive a man to drink. The contrast between the family's aspirations and its poor circumstances suggests that they may have come down in the world. Perhaps the wretched shoemaker, struggling to support his numerous family, felt cut out for better things.

In a letter written when she was in her sixties, Mary indicates that the level of education of the men of the family was certainly beyond that of her father:

> My father was also a "Robert" and was from Buchan and his branch in New Deer and Glenlival and Cabrach, etc. Farmers, one family millers, for generations. The last time I was there, 40 years ago, two sons were at Cambridge, who have gone south. I saw Rev. Alex. Slessor of Aberdeen time before last I was at home. His sons were at the Univ. then in Aberdeen, and one, at least, is a clergyman now, but I have never kept up correspondence with any of them and my own family are all gone long ago . . .

Whatever the reason, Robert Slessor's addiction brought his family into desperate financial straits. Mrs. Slessor, a skilled weaver, had all she could do to keep the growing family fed, clothed and respectable. Yet she did more. Adhering closely to her Church and following with lively interest its pioneering missionary work overseas, she set the dreams of her children on far-off countries where the need for the love of God was even greater than in their own harsh streets.

The eldest son Robert, when still small, was already resolved to be a missionary. The red-haired sister he nick-named "Carrots" and "Fire", to torment her, assisted in make-believe teaching and preaching to dark-skinned listeners (taking a minor part, of course, since she was only a girl). Their Church supported work in China, India, and East Africa but it was the brave new mission venture in Calabar, in tropical West Africa, that particularly enthralled the children. To send Jesus to the poor people of that tortured slave coast was a notion so appealing to the children of Scotland that in the year Mary was born they had, with their groats and halfpennies raised the money for a mission ship, *The Children's Calabar*, whose voyages they could follow in imagination.

But dreams were not enough to sustain the family when the father — decent when sober but no longer reliable — lost his job. By the relentless standards of the Church this was disgrace as well as disaster. They could not look to the eldest son to support the family, for Robert died, as did three of the young Slessors, in childhood.

It was imperative for the women of the family to find steady employment. For this reason, in 1859, they sold up and moved to Dundee where, in the expanding jute mills, there were plenty of jobs, demanding dexterity rather than strength, which could be well and cheaply done by women and children. It was a bitter jest that, in the steep, winding passages around the mills, known as "pends", when the closing bell tolled, it was the men who were at home putting on the kettle for tea. Bitter indeed, because husbands and wives often competed for the same work, which was given to the wives, since women's rates of pay were lower. Then the children suffered.

It is difficult for us to imagine the living conditions of those newly industrialised cities a hundred-odd years ago. The Slessors hoped to make a fresh start, but the change to the crowded, smoky streets of Dundee was a depressing one. The exact location of their first home there is not known for certain. Some think it was Hilltown, some Queen Street. Inevitably the move swallowed up too much of the money realised on their home in Aberdeen, so that their house was sparsely furnished and comfortless. Even the tiny garden became a source of mortification to the children, since their father would insist on digging there on a Sunday, advertising his godlessness to all the world. Poor Bob Slessor couldn't do right!

The harsh statistics of the times help us to imagine what the family faced. The sudden demand for labour had brought into Dundee masses of people with no roots there, to live in wretched, insanitary conditions at bare subsistence level. Illegitimacy was common. Owing to the demand for female workers, families were ill-fed, babies briefly suckled and subsequently neglected. Boys would be employed at good wages until they became men, then be turned adrift in favour of younger children. Cholera, smallpox and typhus were endemic; scarlet fever and diphtheria caused much suffering.

A local historian describes the Dundee of that period:

Being then without the luxury of gaslight, the town was in almost total darkness in the evenings, the only light visible in the streets being dimly burning oil-lamps, widely apart, while the gloom in the wynds and closes was pierced by glinting rays that came through open doors, or chinks in the window shutters of the dwelling houses, from the flickering flame of a candle or "crusey"; while the taverns, chiefly those about the High Street and its vicinity, were filled with cronies or rollicking companions, who sat and gossiped or exchanged news, and laughed or sang over a jug of foaming ale.

But there was another side to Dundee. The people of the town, we are told, were always characterised by religious and devotional habits as well as by independent thinking. Disgusted by the corruption of the clergy, they had been quick to hail the Reformation. George Wishart, its first martyr, had preached to the people from the East Port, now the Wishart Arch, when the town was stricken by plague, while, it is said, John Knox mounted guard to protect him. The Church life of the town was warm and strong.

Robert Slessor found work as a shoemaker and for a time brought home his earnings. Mrs. Slessor entered one of the linen factories, leaving the younger children to the care of Mary. But this was not enough. Mary was still only eleven when she too was sent to work for Baxter Brothers and Company—while the little ones presumably made shift like other children of the poor.

Now life for Mary became a gruelling struggle against physical exhaustion. Though she later described herself as having been "wee and thin and not very strong", and was thought, like others in the family, to be consumptive, she acquired a certain toughness.

Eleven-year-olds were taken into the textile mills as "half-timers", working alternate mornings and afternoons, with lessons the other half-day. One day it would be from six to nine a.m. in the factory, a pause for breakfast, and work again from ten to twelve; then school from twelve-thirty to four. The next day it would be school from nine to twelve-thirty and into the factory from one to six. In winter, when the days were short, it was a very tired child who clattered home in her clogs, dodging as best she could the drunks and ruffians who lurked in the twisting, ill-lit streets.

Yet she began to learn. Three hundred years earlier John Knox had declared that there should be public schools in every parish in Scotland and free education for every child, but when Mary was eleven compulsory schooling was still eleven years in the future and free education not to be enacted for another thirty years. That more than half of the children *were* schooled was thanks to the churches and other charitable institutions. And it was no doubt a mixture of benevolence and self-interest—a pious recognition of what later legislators called the "need of a literate population to maintain the industrial machine"—that caused manufacturers to provide even such rudimentary education as they did for their child workers.

Here, in the half-time school, Mary acquired the three R's and a little music and sewing, knitting and geography. No allowances were made for physical exhaustion. If the weary child couldn't follow the working out of sums on the blackboard she was punished by having to stand till the lesson was finished.

But when she began to work full-time, from six in the morning to six at night, and evening classes replaced the half-time system, her daily schedule became even more punishing. There were still the chores of the home to be fitted in somehow. Yet the hard-won lessons sent a shaft of dazzlement into the dingy slum world. She had, anyway a cheerful nature. Now she could read! There was the Bible and whatever books the Sunday school library could afford. And month by month, like an unfolding serial of exotic adventure, there was the *Missionary Record* that so interested her mother.

Whatever the rigours of the weekday round, on Sunday Mrs. Slessor and her children were to be found neatly dressed in their pew at the Wishart church, near the arch where the martyr had preached. There was a sprinkling of cologne on the children's hand-kerchiefs and gloves and a peppermint each to suck during the sermon. "We would as soon," Mary wrote later, "have thought of going to the moon as of being absent from a service." Here in the friendly church the fatigues and terrors of life could be laid aside. Here was inspiration, learning and decency, and books for the hungry scholar.

By the age of fourteen Mary had become a skilled weaver at a power loom—like her mother one of the better-paid élite of the textile industry. Yet the fortunes of the family went from bad to worse. When Mr. Slessor was in work at all, it was only as a mill labourer. And in 1862 the seventh child of the family, Anne Jane, known as "Janie", was born.

Mary and her mother were driven to shameful exigencies. They were not the only family to bridge the gap between one payday and the next by resorting to the pawnshop—a survey of the times cites mattress tickings, underwear and Waterloo medals as among the pathetic articles pawned—but the Slessors retained a fierce self-respect and suffered cruelly in their pride.

Robert Slessor was caught in the pitiful downward spiral of drink and uselessness. Even if he had sought it, the uplift of the Church was not for him without abject repentance and a reversal of all his ways. But his wife and daughter can have had scant sympathy for him as they struggled to hide the family shame from the younger children and their fellow parishioners. The fear that they might find themselves outcast from the society of Church people was acute. Regularly on Saturday nights, when the little ones were in bed, they braced themselves to face the drunkard's violent homecoming, finding strength in prayer. But the spunky girl undoubtedly tried more direct intervention when her father came home and, lashing about him in sodden rage, threw the precious food her mother had saved for him into the fire. More than once she found herself turned into the cold night street to wander, miserably sobbing, until sleep had stilled his rage and her mother could creep to the door and let her in.

Mrs. Slessor, no fighter perhaps, nevertheless preserved through those bitter years her high standard of conduct and fervent faith. Her headstrong daughter must have found it difficult to acquiesce in the patient resignation that made her mother advise: "Thank God for what you receive; thank God for what you do not receive; thank God for the sins you are delivered from; and thank God for the sins that you know nothing at all about and are never tempted to commit."

She remembered herself as a "wild lassie", full of reckless mischief. She had a tomboy's love of running and jumping and climbing trees and, before she was put to work, enjoyed all the barefoot, grimy, unsupervised freedom of the children of the poor. She was often in trouble for her escapades.

But in stern Calvinist eyes damnation awaited the carefree. An old widow in the district made it her business to call Mary and her friends in off the streets and gather them round her hearth fire, so as to point out to them the dread heat of the flames for which, with their heedless ways, they were surely heading. "If ye dinna repent and believe in the Lord Jesus Christ," she declared, "your souls will burn in the lowin' bleezin' fire for ever and ever!" The words seared into Mary's soul, and with the dramatic suddenness that characterised evangelical religion at that time, her conversion took place, a direct result of the widow's awful warning.

She always claimed that her faith took root then, through shock and fear. But she never tried to manipulate others by a like dread of hell's torments. Fleeing from punishment she discovered — perhaps in the desperate rejection of those Saturday nights locked out in the cold — the deep consciousness of God's nearness and loving care that was the cornerstone of her life. In years to come, she slapped cement on the floor of a mud hut or embarked on a new field of work with equal certainty of divine support. But never did she preach hell-fire in Calabar. Christianity, to her, meant release from the unpredictable terrors of the spirit world, not a fresh bogey-man.

Mary was popular at the linen works, where she proselytised her fellow-workers with shining earnestness. She was warm-hearted, and possessed a dry wit. But if she was seriously courted by any of the factory lads there is no record of it. The scars of childhood may have inhibited thoughts of marriage, for all three of the Slessor girls who survived to womanhood — Mary, Susan, and Janie, remained single. Photographs of Mary show us a decorous young woman in stiff skirt and beribboned bodice, face framed in fashionable cork-screw ringlets. But these are something, one feels, in the nature of a disguise. The look in the eyes is too forthright, the set of the jaw too determined, to go with the bows and lace!

It seems to have been after the death of her father that Mary became actively engaged in home missionary work, though she had always been regular at Bible Class and Prayer Meeting and (with the "impudence of ignorance", as she described it) taught in the Sunday school. So long as her father lived, much of the force of her character went into shielding her family against the worst effects of his drunkenness.

In Mary's lifetime the population of Dundee had more than quadrupled, and about 55,000 people were now engaged in various branches of the linen and jute industry. Around the mills the crooked tenements housed families packed together in every degree of poverty. The women had neither facilities to prepare proper meals nor time to do so. It was in Glasgow that a police superin-tendent said that he could find a thousand children who had no names, or only nicknames, like dogs, but in the demoralising atmosphere of Dundee, with its scarcity of work for men and over-employment of women, the condition of the young can be imagined.

After the death of her father, however, life for Mary's own family was easier. Mrs. Slessor left the factory and kept a small shop where Mary gave a hand on Saturday afternoons and evenings. Her younger brother, John, was growing up and was destined in his turn for the

mission field. All the family loved to be present in the Dundee
churches when missionaries from Africa and the Orient came with
strange, evocative objects to show and stranger stories to tell.
Missionary meetings at this time were a prime entertainment. One
mission secretary begged a worker in Africa to send home such
things as idols, cloth, rattles and calabashes in great quantity since
"notice that such things are to be seen packs a large house on a weekday evening and gives one the opportunity of stating solemn and
important truths".

Today it seems remarkable that the citizens huddled in their
bleak halls should have had compassion — and sixpences — to spare
for beings so distant and little comprehended as those of Africa and
the Orient. But this is to reckon without the overwhelming part
played in their lives by the Church. Surrounded as we are by com-
peting interests we can scarcely conceive how the Church stood
alone in filling the horizons of its flock. When Mary came to consider the rival claims of work in Dundee and overseas, the knowledge
that the people at home were "within sight of church spires and
within hearing of church bells" was the deciding factor. In this the
meanest Scottish orphan seemed to her uniquely privileged.

The returned missionaries begged for workers with every kind of
knowledge and skill. It may have been to satisfy some specific call
that John, frail as he was in health, was apprenticed to the unlikely
trade of blacksmith. While sharing her mother's pride in his dedication, Mary found a worthy field of endeavour closer to hand.

In her early twenties she volunteered as a teacher for the newly
formed Queen Street Mission, close by both church and factory,
which seems to have proved a formidable training ground. The work
was challenging, new, not routine, and this would ever be Mary's
choice. The people served were rough and difficult, for which the
hard disciplines of her own life had prepared her. Although it was
prayer meetings and Bible study classes, not sporting facilities, that
were offered to keep the roughnecks off the street, more than pious
learning was needed to control them. The Mission workers met with
fierce hostility. Mary described how when they went out into the
street after a meeting, the older men used to surround the "smaller
individuals" for their protection. Street gangs amused themselves by
breaking up the meetings. Open-air gatherings were pelted with
mud.

Probably she didn't yet think of herself as a missionary. She was
struggling to complete her own education, reading on her way to
work and, like her idol Livingstone, propping books against the

noisy looms and scribbling odd scraps of knowledge in notebooks. But the city slum was a jungle, though its savages had as fair a complexion as herself. And it decreed its own trial by ordeal.

The Mission workers were supposed to go about the streets in pairs. But Mary never took readily to restrictions. From the dark doorways idle youths, itching for excitement, would watch the small independent figure hurrying past alone in her long dark dress, the carroty hair tucked into a neat bonnet. She was the perfect scapegoat for their resentments, a living reproach to their own lack of purpose. They tried to drive her off, to provoke her with jeers and threats. But she was not to be intimidated.

One night, when she was on her way to conduct a meeting, a gang of young louts set upon her in force, surrounding her and barring her passage. Ominously, the ringleader swung a lump of lead on the end of a cord as he warned her to go away and stop bothering them. The girl refused. If she had learned one thing in those streets, in the mills, in the Saturday nights with a blustering, violent drunk in the home, it was not to show fear.

The lead swung closer, level with her face. She removed her hat (for it was a precious new one decorated with cherries), but the lively blue eyes in the eager boyish face remained determinedly unafraid. The rest of the gang watched in hypnotic silence. Mary prayed inwardly as the weight went round and round, closer and closer until it just missed her forehead; but she would not permit herself to flinch. Suddenly the ringleader threw down his weapon. He had met his match. "She's game, boys!" he cried. And being, it appears, a man of no half measures, he herded his astonished henchmen before him into Mary's prayer meeting.

His words, "She's game, boys!", supreme tribute to courage from the fighting bucks of the northern street-jungle, stand enshrined in the stained-glass window erected to Mary's memory in Dundee.

Another youth tried to make a mockery of her meetings by driving his fellows into them at the crack of a cowhide whip, while himself remaining arrogantly without. One day Mary tackled him on his own ground. "You may whip me", she offered, "if *you* will join the meeting." Uneasily the boy considered the terms of this proposition, looking for the cruel catch that in his experience was always there. Would anyone suffer pain on *his* account? When he saw that she meant what she said and was willing to bear the lash if it would gain her his confidence, his surrender was complete. Once again comes the Revivalist touch: he announced his conversion that very day.

Some of the Church people looked askance at Mary's methods and at the uncouth young creatures she imported into their midst. But behind the challenge Mary laid down to these lads was a genuine delight in their rebellious courage. Cheerfully forgetful of her dignity as a maiden Church worker, she would lead them out on country rambles—secretly delighted, one suspects—for she had a strong streak of devilment in her—by the raised eyebrows of the prim. Her own pent-up spirits soared as she raced the boys across open fields. Her success with them was such that she was invited to undertake similar work in other parts of the city.

Consciously or unconsciously, as she laboured among the poor of Dundee, sitting down to share a meal with no matter what unwashed family, darting into back passageways to knock up her sluggish young adherents and get them to church, she may have found herself repairing a shortcoming in the life of her beloved Church. During her own long struggle to hide her father's weakness from the knowledge of fellow Church people, she must often have hated the respectability which made concealment necessary. But in those days it was her father she blamed. Now, in a sense, she made reparation. There was nothing over-nice or delicate in her conception of Christian duty, no lady-like fear of contamination, no smugness, superiority or scorn.

When a mission superintendent demurred at the "ladies" undertaking to clean a dirty hall, Mary retorted, "We are no ladies, we are just ordinary working folk." At the time of her death it was written of her, "When assisting the poor she sat down among them as one of themselves, with so much tact and sympathy she overcame opposition . . . she stooped low . . . did things others would not have thought of doing."

Yet her sights remained high. She read Milton and Carlyle and Doddridge's *The Rise and Progress of Religion in the Soul*, which had influenced Wilberforce nearly a century earlier. Her own powers of expression unfolded. She began to address devotional meetings outside her own church. As a speaker she was gifted with singular persuasiveness and appeal all her life, but suffered from fits of paralysing shyness. Sometimes it was impossible for her to rise and face her audience and she would whisper what she had to say from her seat. Sometimes she had to beg the men to stow themselves out of sight behind pillars, or leave the room altogether, before she could find her tongue. The urgency of her message, however, would bring her out to speak again, and when she spoke people listened.

Although she was engaged, in Dundee, in what we would call social work, hers was no "social gospel" in our sense. Her theme was that of personal commitment to Christ. Of this she had experience and spoke with authority. A letter written a few years later to one David Stewart, a workmate who may have been one of her mission lads, entreats, "There is *only one Saviour*. He is waiting to be gracious *now*. Pleading with *you*. Oh, if you have not yet settled the palaver that is between you and Him, do so at *once* . . ." And — if not — what will follow? No damnation, it seems, no hell. But for the loving heart hell enough. They will "see each other only as separated friends at the great day". Pale flicker of the old widow's "lowin' bleezin' fire"!

For sixteen years the drudgery at the linen works continued. Mary was eventually so skilled that she could manage two sixty-inch looms at once. The end result was sheeting, sail canvas, salt sacks, tablecloths and towels. Queen Victoria's dish towels, we are told, were of Baxter's linen. Though the floors were greasy with the whale oil used to keep the flax supple, the conditions were not so unpleasant as in the mills where the flax and jute were prepared. In after years she retained pleasant memories. "I am often in the factory, listening to the music of the shuttles, and it is sweet," she tells David Stewart.

But she must have ached to make fuller use of her proven abilities. Certainly she endured a period of perplexity. "If He is to call you to this work, don't wonder if He gives you severe discipline and keeps you long waiting," she wrote to a friend contemplating foreign mission work. "I have passed through deeper waters and darker valleys than you are aware of."

Mary was about twenty-five when her brother John's health broke, and he emigrated to New Zealand in hope of recovery. He died soon after landing. Now there were no sons Mrs. Slessor could dream of setting side by side in glory with the missionaries she so greatly admired.

No sons — but there were daughters. The Calabar Mission with which Mary had, as it were, grown up — her mother had followed every step of its progress since its establishment two years before she was born — had always made use of women workers. Yet it must have been a solemn moment when Mary confessed her desire to go there in her brother's place. For year by year they read in the *Missionary Record* of the hopeful arrivals on the coast known as the "White Man's Grave". And year by year, with tragic regularity, they read the obituaries. Malaria, blackwater fever, yellow fever had

no known cure as yet. They were thought to breed spontaneously
in the miasma of the mangrove swamps. Was Mrs. Slessor to face
the loss of yet another child? No place in the world had so high a
mortality rate for Europeans as had Calabar.

Yet those missionaries believed with ecstatic certainty in death as
the gateway to life everlasting. Mrs. Slessor may well have read an
account by a Jamaican carpenter, of the death in Calabar of his
four-year-old son.

> He went through a burning fever safe to the promised land . . .
> I said, "Keep your bed, you will soon get better." He did get
> better for he was in heaven that same night.

An African, seeing the little boy in his coffin, wept at the sight and
exclaimed, "You missionaries have hearts of iron!" But the child's
father replied, "No, it be God's grace to do all things."

The division between life and a happier life beyond the grave was
thin, and no one, perhaps, was more aware of this than Mrs.
Slessor, whose husband and four children had already passed
through it. She would not stand between her daughter and whatever God's grace held in store.

The death of David Livingstone in 1874 provided the final spur.
All Scotland had been stirred by his travels. The goals he set himself—to abolish the internal slave trade of Africa, to understand the
continent's geography and its water courses, with their enormous
bearing on the resources and lives of the people, to open up Africa to
the Gospel—were well outside the normal pattern of missionary
endeavour. But grand as was his concept of the missionary task, his
sacrificial journeys had one purpose, to carry Christianity into the
heart of Africa. Others must follow where he had led.

Mary's heart quickened at the summons. She began to work out
ways and means, seeking the advice and approval of the men with
whom she had worked in Dundee. Her family could spare her, for
Susan and Janie now had good jobs and she herself should be able
to send money home.

In December 1874, from their home at 17, Harriet Street, Dundee, she made initial inquiries about service in Calabar and was
told: "The branches of education which it is thought desirable for a
female teacher in Old Calabar to possess are those which would
enable her to teach the art of reading in Efik as well as English
and this with the view of giving Bible lessons to the women and
girls." She was urged to improve her education in every way she

could, but particularly with regard to English grammar, and to become "mighty in the Scriptures".

In May 1875 she made formal application for service in Calabar and in December was accepted. She was twenty-seven and had never set foot outside Scotland.

2

WHITE MAN'S GRAVE

PROBABLY NEITHER THE exaltation nor the intransigence of
spirit which were to distinguish Mary Slessor was perceptible in
the fresh-faced young woman who embarked on the steamer
Ethiopia at Liverpool on the 5th August, 1876. Her clothes were
certainly dark, plain and ludicrously unsuitable for the tropics,
since this was the era of trailing skirts, tight sleeves, high necks and
—indispensable to health—something wool next to the skin. Her
only recorded remark to the Dundee friends who saw her off was of
a very proper orthodoxy. As they watched the trade goods loaded
into the hold Mary sighed, "Scores of casks and only one missionary!" What the fever-worn, gin-soaked regulars of the West
African coastal traffic thought (if they overheard) can only be
imagined.

Underlying this simple purposefulness, however, was a shy
friendliness and passionate excitement. After fourteen confining
years at the factory loom, the weaver was now a "female agent" on a
salary of sixty pounds a year (plus twenty-five pounds initial out-
fitting allowance) free, and agog for adventure in the name of Christ.

Three months' training at a normal school—Moray House in
Edinburgh—had been considered sufficient to work this transforma-
tion at a cost to the Mission Board of less than twelve pounds.
Looking back on it, she considered the course to have been too
bookish and not sufficiently practical.

Dr. MacGill, of the Foreign Mission Committee, who had guided
her studies up to the moment of sailing, sent her a last letter of
instructions, pressing upon her the importance of a diligent study
of the Efik tongue. She would be unlikely to forget his words, "You
go not in your own strength . . . Count then prayerfully on His
presence all the way and to the end."

Even today the journey down the west coast of Africa is full of
revelation. After the mists of Biscay and the white light of the
Canary Islands comes the heat and glare of the equatorial ocean. In
the limpid night sky the constellation of the Southern Cross leads

before. By day, porpoises and flying fish break the smooth expanse of ocean. Gradually the long pale skein of the African coastline unravels, with here and there a single palm tree sharp against the sky.

Here it was that the "Old Coaster" traditionally rooted out with his cotton drill jacket and solar topee, spine pad and mosquito boots, his outrageous tales of coast life—of snakes and scoundrels, witchcraft and rough justice—well calculated to unnerve the newcomer. Here, in the coastal ports, African passengers embarked and disembarked, living out their lives on the open deck, cooking, nursing children, bargaining, quarrelling, and displaying a remarkable diversity of physical types.

In Mary's day no traveller went to the Niger coast for pleasure, and few escaped the sense of dread it inspired. For years to come it would be considered one of the deadliest places in the world. Calabar had a particularly unsavoury name. One ship had been known to lose an entire crew twice over through sickness in the months she lay anchored there gathering in cargo.

These were the places to which, in the words of Hope Waddell, founder of the Mission, men went "as though condemned", taking their coffins with them; places for which, as the traveller Mary Kingsley was to find, no return tickets were issued, where death struck frequently, suddenly, and from causes little understood. Yet, though the fascination of its shores was so often literally fatal, men and women continued to come, for the sake of gain, glory, or God— or even, though few would confess it, for the love of Africa itself.

The name Calabar was believed by Harry Johnston, Consul there in the 1880s, to derive from the Portuguese *calabarra*—"the bar is silent". "Old Calabar", he commented, "certainly had a deep and silent bar." In three or four centuries of trade with Europe, it had been witness to strange undertakings.

Calabar was a slaving port throughout the eighteenth and into the nineteenth centuries. On Parrot Island, in the mouth of the Calabar River, when trade was slack, an albino child might be sacrificed as an offering to whatever god brought the great ships of the white man laden with brass rods and brandy, guns and cotton cloth, to barter for that commodity of which there was an endless supply—people. On the slave trade was founded the very considerable prosperity of the four adjacent towns: Creek Town, Duke Town, Henshaw Town, and Old Town, and of their chiefs or kings. The country behind reaped only the ravages of inter-tribal war and slave raids.

The long commerce between trading ships and the city-states

which controlled the waterways of the Delta had produced coastal societies of a curious sophistication. Trade English was widely spoken and even written, as shown by a strange surviving document, a portion of a diary written by an early Efik trader, Antera Duke, in the years 1785–1788.* Antera Duke's diary gives an eerie insight into the dealings between African traders and European captains on ship and shore. Entries concerning trade ("Captain Tatam went away with 395 slaves") alternate with comment on the weather ("There was a little morning rain") and such ritual observances as sacrifice for the dead ("We hear that Tom Robin's family have cut men's heads off for young Tom.") Precise social notations ("At seven o'clock at night I have all the Captains to supper at my house") and routine domestic preoccupations ("I go on board the Fairweather to fetch his joiner to make windows for my big house") jostle bizarre family palavers: "All Captain John's family came to see us about one of their daughters who married Egbo Young and had fought with another wife and broken her teeth out. We made Jimmy Antera take out the teeth of the wife, the daughter of Ephraim Robin Henshaw." "We drank all day until night" is a typical entry, the drink being sometimes the local *mimbo*, or palm wine, but just as frequently imported brandy.

This was the life of Calabar sixty years before any white man lived among the people. Power was wielded by men of substance through the agency of the secret Egbo (or Ekpe) Society, to the highest grades of which all the richest men belonged. Women and slaves, who had no share in the Society's mysteries, went in particular dread of the "Egbo" members since to catch sight of them even by accident could result in stripping, scourging or death. Chiefs could be ostracised and cut off from trade-dealings by having Egbo "blown" on them or their houses, and English traders could be boycotted in the same way. "So we sent Ekpe drum to blow", Antera Duke says, "forbidding everyone in the town to come or go to market."

In the hands of this small oligarchy were accumulated large quantities of—frequently useless—European articles of trade. European-style houses were shipped out from Liverpool and erected more for prestige than accommodation. They can be seen to this day furnished with dining tables that would seat thirty or forty people

* Extracts reprinted by permission of the International African Institute from the Diary of Antera Duke in *Efik Traders of Old Calabar*, edited by Daryll Forde, London, Oxford University Press for International African Institute, 1956. Reprinted by Dawsons of Pall Mall, London, 1968.

for occasions when the chiefs entertained the "river gentlemen" at feasts of palm oil "chop" washed down with neat spirits.

But European importations did little to alter the life and customs of the ordinary people. No white men lived ashore, and there was little in the slaver's life at sea to inspire envy or emulation. It is doubtful if European captains, filling their ships' holds with their wretched human cargo, were hypocritical enough to protest against the ritual sacrifice of slaves on shore. They could hardly have been unaware of the killing that, according to Antera Duke, took place to mark the obsequies of one Duke Ephraim.

About 4 a.m. I got up; there was great rain, so I walked to the town palaver house and I found all the gentlemen there. So we got ready to cut heads off and at 5 o'clock in the morning we began to cut slaves' heads off, fifty heads off in that one day. I carried 29 cases of bottled brandy, and 15 calabashes of chop for everybody, and there was play (dancing and mime) in every yard in town.

They must also have known about trial by ordeal, usually by administering a potion made from the poisonous esere (or Calabar) bean. The innocent were expected to vomit and recover.

We hear that King Aqua has made all his wives drink doctor. So 11 wives died from drinking doctor ...

By the mid-nineteenth century, when the first missionaries came, Calabar was in many respects unchanged. But the population had become increasingly demoralised by its long dependence on the slave-trade. Slaves made up the bulk of the population, living in varying degrees of dependence on the families of the great trader-chiefs. An Efik "house" including all dependents, slave and free, often numbered up to a thousand persons. King Eyo Honesty, in 1847, was reckoned to have *thousands* of slaves and 400 canoes with a captain and crew for each one. Except for his precarious tenure of life, the domestic slave differed little from the freeman. He was rarely sold or mistreated. But the ceremonial killing which was clearly limited by custom in Antera Duke's day had now overreached all bounds. As each house tried to outdo the other in the extravagance of the retinue provided for their eminent dead, wives, concubines and slaves might be indiscriminately strangled, drowned and shot in their hundreds on the death of an important chief. The more responsible chiefs were themselves disturbed by the orgies of blood-letting that occurred.

Yet as the slave traffic was displaced by trade in palm oil, there

developed, in spite of these excesses, a problem of surplus population. So it was that, in 1845, on yielding to British pressure to sign a
final agreement not to export slaves, the chiefs of Creek Town and
Duke Town entreated the commander of the naval vessel to help
them find new ways to make use of their manpower. King Eyamba of
Duke Town wrote:

> ... Now we can't sell slave again, we must have too much man for
> country, and want something to make work and trade, and if we
> could get seed for cotton and coffee we could make trade. Plenty
> sugar cane live here, and if some man can teach me way for do it,
> we get plenty sugar too; and then some man must come for teach
> book proper, and make all men saby God like white man, and
> then we go on for same fashion.

He and King Eyo Honesty of Creek Town, who wrote in similar
vein, had probably heard of the new missionary enterprises on the
Niger, and at Badagry and Lagos to the west. For when the Jamaica
Mission Presbytery, which had come to feel a concern for Africa
through its work with the freed slaves of the West Indies, proposed
settling and working in Calabar, eight kings and chiefs readily put
their hand to an agreement to grant them land and protection, welcoming the missionaries' coming and "hoping to have their children
taught in English learning".

In 1846 the Calabar Mission was established by the Rev. Hope
Waddell and a small company which included several West Indians.
Calabar was lucky, for they came well-informed about Africa,
adjusted to tropical living and in a spirit of humble reparation for
the evils of the slave-trade.

There were to be times when the kings and chiefs would wish they
could restrict the newcomers to the instilling of those minimal
educational skills that would enable their sons to meet foreign
traders on fair ground, and be spared their tendency to general interference. But by and large they supported the Mission's work, even
if in dilatory fashion. The Calabar that Mary Slessor found in 1876,
for all its unsavoury reputation, was a safer, seemlier place than that
of thirty years before. Where life had been so uncertain that no one
thought of planting a tree, the Mission gardens bloomed with fruit
and flowers.

The missionaries had taught and cajoled the Calabar people from
highest to lowest, produced a dictionary and books in the Efik
language, explored the hinterland, and waged a running battle
against the most cruel and highhanded practices of the powerful

ruling caste. It was an uphill struggle. In 1850 ten captains, three surgeons and two missionaries formed "A Society for the Suppression of Human Sacrifices in Calabar" and secured the pledge of the Creek Town and Duke Town kings that no human being would be killed except for crime. The Egbo Society, which acted as a kind of police force in the Efik towns, was also persuaded to enact a law to this effect. Lip service, at least, began to be paid to the new order of things.

On the other hand, the missionaries had not had it all their own way. The Calabar people had been dealing for centuries with white men, of whom the noble and gallant were few beside the mercenaries and hirelings — greedy, sick, often cruel and embittered, sojourners on that hated coast. They were not to be bowled over by the wonder of a white face. The missionaries had to prove their worth and usefulness.

When Hope Waddell, the founder of the Mission, first expounded the ten commandments in Creek Town, King Eyo Honesty (so named because of his scrupulous dealings with foreign merchants) energetically approved or objected to each one in turn, and the eighth commandment — *Thou shalt not steal* — provoked a general burst of satirical laughter. One can feel for the king confronted for the first time by the doctrine of the final resurrection:

"All them old people that died long time, will they all live again?" the king exclaimed. "Them old bones that rot in the ground. How will God raise them up again? Where will they live? The world can't hold them." The last judgment and doom of the wicked startled him. The congregation was very attentive and solemnised during the latter part of my address, and when I concluded with prayer the king said "This be very good meeting. I like we have this every Sunday." Adverting to the sixth commandment, he remarked, "You say man no for kill. True. What use a man take his money go buy slave, and then kill him for nothing? If he have too many men for his work, let him stop buy. But slaves be too bad." I replied that if the word of God restrained the masters, it would also improve the slaves, and make them both better to each other. "Well, I hope so," he answered; and so concluded our first meeting.

The Rev. William Anderson, whose sermon in Dundee had first fired Mrs. Slessor's interest in Calabar a quarter of a century earlier, told of preaching, "after some deed of blood," that at the last trump murderers and murdered would rise together for God's judgment when: "King Archibong I jumped up in fury — 'We go now' — and hurried off . . . H. Cobham cried out 'That plenty today'; and Mr. Young said in his softest manner 'That do for today, Mr. Anderson; you come back next Sunday and tell us all about it.' And thus my congregation dismissed me that day . . ."

Perhaps the outstanding feat of the missionaries was to have established permanent homes in the White Man's Grave. Until they did so the only white men to remain ashore at Calabar were the dead. And while they may not have proved conclusively that "life could be lived there without fear, rum or fever", as Hope Waddell had hoped they should, a visiting deputy of the Church was hardly exaggerating when he described the missionary home with its "refined and orderly ways" as "one of the most effective of missionary instrumentalities . . . an exhibition of civilisation . . . a public declaration for righteousness and protest against iniquity . . . a mind, a conscience and a heart to the land."

The effect was the greater in that, from the beginning, each mission house took in large numbers of unwanted or orphaned children and raised them up in its ways. Moreover, it was home from home to many of the traders, helping to bridge the often wide divergence of view between missionary and merchant on matters of public policy and private conduct.

The "gentlemen of the river" were no longer seamen only. With the expansion of the palm oil trade, ships remained a whole season in the river, waiting for the palm oil to filter down from the inland markets. And when trading firms introduced the practice of bringing out old hulks of ships and mooring them in the rivers as floating warehouses and homes for the supercargoes it meant that the factors, coopers and clerks no longer travelled home with each shipment of oil. Great numbers of them died of fever, but the river was held to be cooler and healthier than the shore (as well as safer, no doubt, from breaches of the eighth commandment!) This was the situation when Mary landed in September, 1876. The hulks, roofed over with matting like great floating barns and swinging in the tide below Duke Town, must have been among her first impressions. As the river broadened into a basin surrounded by palm-covered hills, and the *Ethiopia* threaded its way among shipping and canoes to its anchorage, she was probably pleasantly surprised that the shore should present a picture of such charm. Jesse Hogg, a later arrival, saw it like this:

Duke Town comes in sight suddenly, round a bend, after a sail of between forty and fifty miles from the mouth of the river. You

could not see a prettier picture than Duke Town, on a fine day,
set off with its tropical greenery. The native town lies in a hollow,
with a background of high cotton trees. Its mat-roofed mud huts
are relieved by a few gaily-painted wooden houses belonging to
the King and Chiefs. The steamer anchors in full view of the
town, mission and Consulate. Boats with white awnings, manned
by kru boys (men from another part of the coast, who do the
heavy work) in white singlets, red caps and dark loin-cloths, come
alongside. The Captain holds quite a reception, for the coming of
the fortnightly steamer is an event.

Very soon we are in the mission gig, and six strong kru boys,
with a long pull and a strong pull, make the boat glide delightfully
through the water to the mission beach . . .

The mission is reached after a climb. The whitewashed
church, school, dispensary, mission houses, are all in a cluster,
amid a profusion of orange, bread-fruit, mango, plantain and
banana trees.

Miss Hogg goes on to tell of the airy frame houses "where the
white people all live on the upper flat", and of the black children
dressed up to meet the new arrival. "They speak in an unknown
tongue, but they show their white teeth and look delighted. This
kindly reception from the children of the mission house gives a good
impression of the people."

The principal work of the Mission was being done at Creek Town
and Duke Town, within signalling distance of one another across the
Calabar River, with lesser stations at Old Town and further up the
Cross River at Ikorofiong. When Mary arrived there was a staff of
twelve Europeans (not counting wives) one ordained African and
eighteen African agents. The avowed aim (to quote the Rev. Hugh
Goldie) was "not to evangelise the various tribes of Africa but to
raise up a native agency to do so".

The Mission's desire to train up an Efik-speaking body of
Christians to carry on the work ran, however, directly counter to the
chiefs' desire to have their children learn just enough commercial
English and mathematics for purposes of trade. Church attendance
was large but, as the practice of polygamy and slave ownership were
both universal and unacceptable to the Church, membership was
meagre. When William Anderson surveyed the work of twenty-five
years, he concluded that "the thousands still unimpressed, unin-
terested and uninstructed".

The most notable achievement had been in the social field.

Emboldened by missionary teachings, the slave class had formed a covenant for their mutual protection against sacrificial slaughter. This mass movement, known as the "Blood Men", came to rival Egbo in power and had considerable success in safeguarding the lives of its adherents.

Mary was to become one of the Anderson household and teach in the Duke Town school. But the Andersons were on leave at the time of her arrival. In charge was a comparative newcomer, the Rev. Alexander Ross. There were also Alexander Morton, a teacher, and Mrs. Sutherland, a veteran in the field of women's work, Mrs. Ross and Mrs. Morton.

Women agents had been described by the Foreign Mission Board as "economical and effective", surely an understatement in the case of Euphemia Sutherland, Mary's new mentor. She had gone to Calabar as a young woman, married a fellow missionary and survived his early death to work on for twenty-seven years. Even that ageing dynamo, William Anderson, declared himself unfit for the round of work Mrs. Sutherland set herself. She taught in the school each morning and in the afternoon visited the women in the "yards", or women's quarters, dosing ailments, instructing in housecraft and needlework, vaccinating against smallpox, and setting husbands to rights too, it would appear from her own good-natured account:

> ... the men do not expect to be passed by. So they, too, get the benefit of a short lecture before I go among their wives, which I must say, they all take in good part. The worst word I get from them is "Well, Mammy, it is hard for me to begin new fashion." When told it is not a new fashion of man's making but the word of God, which God himself told them to adopt, the next answer is "True, Mammy, I will try". This is sometimes said by way of getting off!

The *Record* soon reported that Miss Slessor had "entered with strong hope and courage" on her labours as a female teacher at Duke Town and was a "promising daughter" to Mrs. Sutherland. Hope and courage were needed. Mary was appalled by the conditions she found. "We may *read* and *hear*," she wrote shortly, "but to *see* the state of society here is sickening ... I never thought that my sense of delicacy would be so far blunted. The scenes we cannot speak or write of ..."

Yet her extraordinary round of work became routine and she prefaced an account of one Sunday in the company of Mrs. Sutherland with the words, "I have nothing at all new or wonderful to write, for

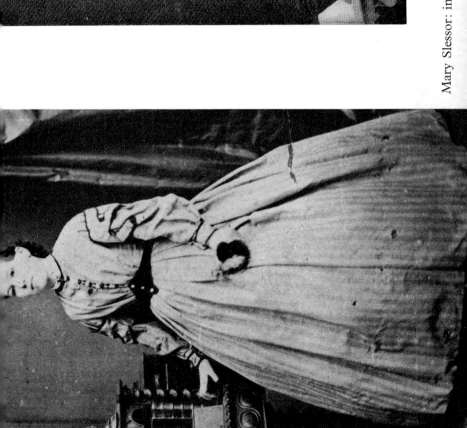

Mary Slessor: in youth and early middle age

Dundee: King Street leading up to Baxter's Mill

17, Harriet Street, Mary's home in 1875

anything novel or out of ordinary seldom comes in my way." Each encounter, of that day, however, pointed to some weakness in the social fabric and nearly all underlined the indignities womankind suffered in a polygamous society.

They began with a futile attempt to convince a group of rum-sellers of the error of their ways.

Here the usual question is asked in the usual triumphant fashion. "What for white man bring them rum, suppose them rum be no good? He be god-man he bring them rum, what for god-man talk so?"

They found a family in mourning, unwashed, and unkempt, as the custom was. In another compound Mary tried to comfort a father bitterly convinced that his dead child had been "witched". She entered the "fatting house" where, by tradition peculiar to the Calabar region, girls were kept in seclusion, fattened by heavy food, and prepared by the old women for marriage.

They visited a household of women recently widowed, where the "senior" wife sat "like a repulsive, mediaeval witch", surrounded by skulls and charms, tormenting the wretched younger wives of their late lord and master. Yet when Mary joined a group of self-declared Christian women she was depressed by their complacent piety and returned to Mission Hill tired and heavy-hearted.

She mastered the Efik tongue quickly, so quickly it astonished everyone. The Africans declared she was blessed "with an Efik mouth". Plunged daily into the company of the women, who were less adept than the men at "trade" English, she picked it up by ear with unprecedented ease.

Her fluency gave her a great advantage with the children who — regardless of the chiefs' opposition — were taught in the vernacular at infant level, and it also gave her an early insight into the mentality of the people.

She had imagined Africa to be without religion and without God. Now she found that the interaction of unseen forces with the visible world was often more strongly felt than in Europe. "Every man knows," the first King Eyo had said, "that God lives, and that he made all things." The notion of *Abassi*, the supreme God, presented no difficulty. But there were hosts of unseen spirits, malevolent or capricious, to be guarded against, or enlisted to serve one's own ends. Every custom and observance of life had to do with the placating and searching out of these mysterious forces, which could be neglected only at peril.

Before long, Mary was sent on a tour of the Mission stations, travelling by river, and on foot, through the dense palm forest, assisted by three canoe boys. In some places the unaccustomed sight of a white face would send the children screaming to their mothers, but Mary found the people more engaging than the hybrid population of the town. Though the conquest of the interior regions was scarcely held to be the work of the Mission's female staff, it is likely that Mary already conceived it to be hers. Only a month after she had reached Calabar she was writing, "one does need a special grace to enable one to sit still. It is so difficult to wait."

But wait she must. By January Louisa Anderson was back in Calabar, and her rigorous hand lay over the pattern of days. Up at five, stern and methodical, she roused the household and set them about their tasks. At prayers, twice a day, she expected the house-children to answer questions and repeat portions of Scripture. A stickler for promptness in a place where clocks were scarcely known, she was also large of heart and mothered not only countless aban-doned children but many young white traders, nursing them through illness in her own house. Called "the silent", she could soften the effects of "Daddy" Anderson's robust tempers—though it was he who smuggled food to Mary when, as often happened, she was late for meals and should, by the rule of the house, have gone hungry.

The effect of her example on the receptive newcomer can hardly be exaggerated. "Mammy" Anderson had been known to disarm a thief of his matchet and send him packing. She built houses, marked out roads and castigated chiefs, and she had been doing these things for nearly thirty years. One old chief, amazed by her industry, is said to have declared, "I tell you true, them woman be best man for mission!"

Accustomed as she was to the discipline of unremitting labour, Mary Slessor was too impetuous to take easily to living by rule. Sharply reproached by Mrs. Anderson for oversleeping when it was her task to get up and ring the rising bell, she began anxiously waking and stumbling out while it was yet moonlight. Though the climate was not one to produce an excess of energy (". . . here we cannot spend so much strength as at home"), Mary's high spirits were so stifled in the Mission that she claimed to have climbed every tree worthy of the name between Duke Town and Old Town. In ankle-length skirts at the age of twenty-nine!

It may have been only her comparative youth and a touch of home-sickness that made her write, "I feel the solitariness of my position a little more than I expected . . ." or she may have felt the lack of that elaborately regulated domestic background that the ministers' wives possessed. Even the kindly ex-slave, Mrs. Fuller, who had first come from the West Indies as a children's nurse, would have known a more spacious way of life than she.

Yet she was deeply devoted to her first preceptors, and twenty-five years later wrote with a rush of nostalgia of the "romantic Old Calabar of my youth! The dear old friends, whose like we do not see now. The changed conditions from the days when we lived among the natives, and they and we were free as the air to pursue callings under more than Bohemian licence, the advent of the steamers with their old and kindly, if rather rough and exaggerated, criticisms from skipper and man, the open hospitality on hulk and in Mission houses, and the general camaraderie and bond of friendship, which a stay on this coast invariably conveyed."

At the time, however, she wrote to a friend of her factory days, David Stewart, "I am now, as you know, among quite a different class of people from that I was accustomed to at home. The European Society apart from the members of the Mission are merchants, the government officials, the commanders, doctors and pursers of the Steamers, Travellers, Botanists, Explorers, etc. etc. But" — she adds a trifle wearily — "though I value the refinement, education, etc. of such society, I hope to be in fair with the dear old friends at home."

The open-handed hospitality of the Mission, such a boon to the lonely traveller, or the trader living his unnatural life on the river hulks, may well have been a burden for Mary. On those Sunday evenings after the English-language service, when the Europeans gathered for tea at the Andersons' invitation before descending the steep hill to their boats, the social niceties so appreciated by a gentlemanly ship's captain may well have seemed tedious and irrelevant to the ex-mill girl.

In her contacts with the Calabar people, however, Mary's shyness vanished. She became fast friends with King Eyo VII of Creek Town. According to Sir Harry Johnston, British Consul in 1887, King Eyo was "a Christian, the husband of one wife, and a thoroughly European man, who spoke, read and wrote excellent English, always dressed in European clothes, lived in a European house and was a thoroughly estimable character" — at least, by European standards! This progressive, handsome chief, delighted to hear of her mother's interest in him, wrote Mrs. Slessor a letter, entering into a correspondence that would certainly be of deep human interest if it had survived.

Mary worked hard, dividing her time between the school and women's yards, but put on weight. When her thirtieth birthday caught up with her she was at pains to remind herself that she was growing "an *old woman*", but added: "Really, among my bairns I am like to forget the fact, for I am as young in spirit yet as ever I was. And some of the Europeans were telling me lately that I am growing younger and better looking. This means that I am better in health for after an African fever one looks as if one had escaped from a lunatic asylum."

Frequent attacks of fever were, however, inevitable. The cause of malaria was still not understood and she could only pray for strength to withstand its periodic onslaughts and dose herself with quinine when it came. On one occasion at least, Mary was seriously ill, and she was run-down in health and longing for home by the time she sailed on furlough in June 1879.

3

TO CHANGE THE CUSTOMS

ALREADY, DURING HER first home leave, Mary was talking of her wish to work among the inland tribes of Calabar—with the reputedly fierce Okoyong, or in the inaccessible Oban Hills. Her imagination was haunted by the needs of the "untouched multitudes" who still lived (her phrase) "in the seat of Satan".

Her impatience was shared to some extent by the home Church. For a Mission field so wasteful of human life as Calabar had been, the achievement there seemed small. Little progress had been made towards the Livingstonian goal of opening the way for Christianity into the heart of Africa. But, though the Foreign Mission Committee were pressing the Calabar Presbytery to "open a back door into the interior", Mary was not soon to have her way.

The senior members of the Mission were elderly. For thirty-odd years they had seen the men and women who might have led the way forward arrive, work for a time, fall sick, and die or be invalided home. There had been no lack of eager explorers, but new stations had often to be abandoned before the mud dried on the first buildings, because blackwater fever or dysentery robbed them of a guiding hand. In conditions so hostile to European life the old men of the Mission deemed it best to concentrate their efforts on Calabar, on educating an African ministry of the future, and were not enthusiastic about new adventures inland.

Mary, however, showed no signs of settling down to the life of a Duke Town teacher. On returning to Africa she requested any post but Duke Town.

She travelled back in the company of that gentle old scholar, tireless teacher and translator, Hugh Goldie, whose Efik dictionary and Bible are still standard works today. His wife was with him. We cannot know how much their journey allowed them to see of the scope of other missions along the coast—where Methodists, Anglicans, French Catholics and American Baptists were all now at work—but such glimpses could well have increased Mary's restlessness. Few Churches confined themselves to so narrow a sphere as did the Presbyterians.

On arrival at Calabar she found to her pleasure that she was to be placed in charge at Old Town, three miles along the Calabar River, to work virtually alone except for the help of a young Efik woman and several boys and girls who would live with her for training.

Old Town had had an uneven history. Although it was one of the four towns where Hope Waddell began work in 1846, its chief, Willy Tom Robins, held firmly to the ways of his forefathers and resisted all change. In his last illness, in defiance of consul, Mission, sea captains and the reformed Egbo law, he had wives, sons, slaves and freemen chained up as hostages. On his death they were shot, hanged and poisoned.

This blood bath stirred fierce indignation among the "river gentlemen" who persuaded the acting consul to employ the then customary method of instilling right-thinking into native populations, i.e. to bring up a gunboat and shell the town. Overriding the protests of the missionaries, Consul Lynslager evacuated the inhabitants and had the place razed to the ground.

Though rebuilt a few years later, Old Town was never again more than a backwater. Sporadic efforts by the Mission, mainly in the person of Mrs. Sutherland, had met with little response. The Mission house—a temporary one of mud and palm-thatch—was often vacant and had fallen into disrepair.

Mary had a particular reason for wanting to go there. During her year at home she had moved her mother and sisters into healthier surroundings at Downfields, on the outskirts of Dundee. This meant sending them more of her salary, but she believed she could live very cheaply if allowed to do so. Local produce—the tiny tough chickens, river fish, yams, maize, beans, fruit and palm oil—cost next to nothing compared with imported commodities like flour, tea, sugar, butter and bacon. Moreover, they provided an acceptable diet, were available in local markets, and could be prepared by African girls without much supervision.

Mary did not broadcast her reasons for choosing to live in this way, and was regarded as highly eccentric. But she did not believe in sacrifice for its own sake. Plain living was forced upon her. Yet who is to say that, brought up as she had been, she really minded? There was none of that model housekeeping and gracious entertaining so dear to the hearts of other mission ladies. The wealthy chiefs did not give *her* their daughters to train. But it was at Old Town that Mary's pattern of life took shape.

There, as in Dundee, she sat down among the people "as one of themselves". When, later in her life, it was said that "living very close to the natives she entered into their thought, learned intricate family relationships, and acquired patience and decision necessary to influence them", it was partly because at Old Town, in 1880, she lacked money to do otherwise.

Her work was now immensely varied. In addition to supervising the three informal schools for all ages at Old Town and its neighbouring villages of Qua and Akim, she dispensed simple medicines, tried to train her houseful of youngsters to usefulness in the home and schools, and mediated in local disputes. There were always abandoned children to be looked after. In view of the curious willingness of the "God-men" to undertake the care of children not their own, unwanted babies were frequently dumped at the mission gate.

On Sundays she preached at small gatherings for many miles around, trudging from one hamlet to another throughout the day. Two boys, carrying a pole on which a bell was slung, marched before to summon the congregation, while Mary visited the sick and routed out the reluctant. As darkness fell, she returned to Old Town and gathered her own flock together in the chief's compound for a more formal service by lamplight, to which most of the community came.

Conditions at Old Town differed little from those in the "bush" beyond, where a scattered peasant population, mostly slaves, worked the farms belonging to the great traders.

The word "bush" requires some explanation here. One cannot write of West Africa without it. It may mean all wild, uncultivated rural places, or one particular such area. It describes not so much a particular type of land as a remote quality of life, and may equally indicate forest, scrubland or swamp. The "bush" is all that is not urban or suburban. The "bush man" is a yokel, a rustic bumpkin, a peasant.

The bush immediately behind Old Town, near as it was to the coast, contained a life remote and separate. Rev. J. K. Macgregor, harking back to this period, wrote:

> Every village had a feud with its neighbour . . . A man did not dare in those early days to go alone along the paths through the bush. Even when going for water to the springs the women took their lives in their hands. Besides the spirits that were supposed to dwell in the bush and molest people, any tree might have behind it a foe of flesh and blood.

Regardless of real or imagined dangers, Mary began to go farther and farther afield. Her Old Town congregation viewed these excursions with alarm. The rain forest is eerie as well as beautiful and it is easy to lose one's bearings, particularly in a sudden storm. There are snakes and scorpions scuttling in the undergrowth, poisonous centipedes, leeches, and jiggers that work in between the toes. By night it is a tumult of mysterious sound, from the croaking of frogs and hoot of nightjar, the throbbing of drums and uncanny voice of gourd flutes, to the growl of leopards and bang of the hunter's gun. Mary owned that the danger was real, but said, "He has promised that we can take up serpents, why should I be afraid of leopards?" and claimed that she frequently went her way through the darkness praying aloud, "Oh God of Daniel, shut their mouths!" "And He did!" she would add. If she had canoe men or carriers with her she kept them singing, secure, it seems, in the certainty that the resultant caterwauling would scare off "any decent, respectable leopard!"

The narrow paths that led out of each village on to the next drew her irresistibly forward. She soon ceased to care where night found her or what shelter offered. Except for a "chop box" containing essential supplies of bread and tea she took little with her but the medical bag which every missionary carried and which often served as her introduction.

Her cures, like those of the native doctors, must have owed much to faith. Later she became something of an expert on native herbs but at this time she had no training whatever and must have relied heavily on poultices of bread or boiled yam, all-purpose medicines like quinine and epsom salts, and pain-killers like laudanum. Even the learned Hope Waddell, however, who had held daily "clinics" in Calabar, had relied only partly on the contents of his medicine chest. "Use no native medicine, employ no native doctor, drink no rum, pray to Jesus for a blessing, and praise Him for recovery", was his advice to patients.

Mary's ministrations established sympathy among strangers. By the bush paths, in the market, on the river bank, as she bathed and bandaged, lanced boils and dosed for constipation, she spoke to young and old, slave and free, leper and widow, of the love of Christ for *them*. This was the work she loved best. Her insistence on a personal caring God, combined with her own gentle touch, came as a heady draught to those humble men and women, many of them of the slave class, accustomed to think of themselves as ever forfeit to the demands of tradition and custom.

The destruction of Old Town twenty years earlier had not in the least disposed of its brutal customs. Many of these bore hardest on the women. Working intimately with them as she did, Mary encountered in all its pathos one of the least defensible of all practices, that of twin-murder.

The horror of twins felt in Calabar seems to have rested on the mystical belief that one of the children was the offspring of an evil spirit. As it could not be determined which, both were usually destroyed. Their backs were broken and they were pushed alive into clay pots, or thrown on to an ant hill, or into the bush, to die.

The mother, thought to have had intercourse of unnatural kind and given birth to abomination, was regarded, and regarded herself, with abhorrence. She became an outcast, shunned by husband and family and forbidden to contaminate with her presence any house or path which others might use. Special villages existed for these miserable women which, understandably — since the women could not leave or follow any occupation — became places of ill-fame. One cannot stress enough the strength of this taboo. The ultimate curse on any woman was to hold up two fingers signifying "May you have twins!" The ultimate insult for a man was to declare that he was "such as would be willing to marry a twin woman". Intercourse with a "twin woman" was in some places punishable by death. D. Amaury Talbot went so far as to declare:

> Sad indeed is the lot of girl twins rescued from the fate ordained by the law of their race; for, unless some fortunate chance takes them away from their own country, they are shunned through life. No matter where they may strive to hide their secret it somehow gets known that they are "twin women" and no man would dream of approaching such with thoughts of love and marriage save those who have absolutely no regard for their reputations.

It is hard to see, however, how Christian missionaries could have done otherwise than give these tiny mites a chance of life. From the earliest days the missionaries and their wives flew to the rescue whenever they heard rumour of a twin birth. Mrs. Sutherland described how, when the first twins were carried through the market, the women scattered at the sight of the basket and of the mother, one clapping her hands over her ears and crying, "Don't let me hear; am dead, am dead, am dead, oh!"

Every Mission home had its complement of twin babies, usually looked after in the house itself, since even in the surrounding compound they were not safe. For the children there was some hope. Fear of them diminished as they grew up in apparent normality.

But their mothers too often became permanent hangers-on in the mission compounds.

Twins were not the only babies in need of rescue. Similar taboos applied to the children of any abnormal birth, and slave children whose mothers died in giving them birth were often thrown away, as no one could be troubled to rear them.

For a single-handed missionary, the children were a job in themselves, and from Old Town Mary proposed to the Foreign Mission Committee that a woman should be appointed solely for the purpose of caring for them. "If such a crowd of twins should come to her as I have to manage, she would require to devote her whole time to them." But she was ahead of her time. Practical projects such as this were slow to find favour, and this one did not take shape for several decades.

Widows were hardly better off than the mothers of twins. If not required to stand trial by ordeal for the death of their husbands by witchcraft, they were secluded with their heads shaven, sometimes for years, in filth and semi-starvation. According to *Nigeria* magazine,

> Some were imprisoned in tiny, unventilated cells and kept deliberately in a state of filth so that they might become filled with every sort of vermin. Some women were covered by layers of cow dung or itching leaves so that they became tormented, scratching demons. All this, it should be said, among a people of very cleanly habits. "Weeping exhibitions" were held at which women were submitted to public beatings which ended when there was no point in going on.

Among the treaties agreed with Calabar chiefs by successive British consuls was one signed in 1878, which decreed a penalty of death for any who took the life of a twin child or children, as well as punishment for their accomplices. Human sacrifice was made punishable by death, as was the administration of the poison ordeal, *whether the person taking it died or not*. Persons voluntarily undergoing the ordeal in order to exonerate themselves from guilt, were subject to fines and banishment. The seclusion of widows was abolished and the mourning period restricted to one month. Furthermore, the "abominable, disgraceful and barbarous custom" of allowing the young men of the town to take an Ekpo out, and seize, strip, and indecently assault any women wearing a dress or cloth in the street was "forever abolished". Hopeful words!

In a vivid letter to Sunday school children in Dundee, Mary

described the reception of the news of this new edict by the mothers and children in her care:

> Just as it became dark one evening I was sitting in my verandah talking to the children, when we heard the beating of drums and the singing of men coming near. This was strange, because we are on a piece of ground which no one in the town has a right to enter. Taking the wee twin boys in my hands I rushed out, and what do you think I saw? A crowd of men standing outside the fence chanting and swaying their bodies. They were proclaiming that all twins and twin-mothers could now live in the town, and that if any one murdered the twins or harmed the mothers he would be hanged by the neck. If you could have heard the twin-mothers who were there, how they laughed and clapped their hands and shouted "Sosono! Sosono!" (Thank you! Thank you!) you will not wonder that amidst all that noise I turned aside and wept tears of joy and thankfulness, for it was a glorious day for Calabar.
>
> A few days later the treaties were signed and at the same time a new King was crowned. Twin-mothers were actually sitting with us on a platform in front of all the people. Such a thing had never been known before. What a scene it was! How can I describe it? There were thousands of Africans, each with a voice equal to ten men at home, and all speaking as loudly as they could. The women were the worst. I asked the Chief to stop the noise. "Ma", he said, "how I fit stop them women mouth?" The Consul told the King that he *must* have quiet during the reading of the treaties, but the King said helplessly "How can I do? They be women — best put them away," and many *were* put away.

She goes on to describe the silks and satins, plumes and bangles, beadwork and painted masks, braid and bells that were worn by the people for this great occasion, a reminder of how well-off were the trading people of the coast compared with their brothers inland.

In one of Mary's Bibles, by the verse in Acts that goes: "This Jesus of Nazareth . . . shall change the customs" are inscribed the words, "Yes, thank God!" It was a cry from the heart.

Certain changes for the better followed immediately on the signing of the treaty. In the following year Mrs. Sutherland reported that twin-mothers could walk about the towns and go to market and the widows of even such an important man as Archibong II displayed with pride their "nice, plaited hair".

But women in rural areas were not much touched by these reforms. Mary began pressing the case for special work with them. It was not enough to introduce legislation to stop the men misusing them. The women had to be brought to reject their own low status. This proposal too, remained in abeyance.

Meanwhile, at Old Town and Qua, and on trips along the river, Mary began to mull over another problem that had plagued European traders and administrators for years—the tight monopoly which the powerful middlemen of the coast held over trade with foreign merchants. No farmer wishing to market his produce could sell direct to the European "factories" without the Calabar traders intervening to exact duty from both—payments known picturesquely as "shake-hands" or "comey". Such was the stranglehold over commerce, and the terror in which the Calabar war canoes were held, that the up-river tribes had little incentive to grow or produce anything for sale.

Characteristically, Mary took action. When the Qua people were at war with the Efik and so had no outlet for their palm kernels, the injustice of the position so stirred the blood of the once-wild Scots lassie that she herself would lead anyone with produce to sell over mission land by night, past the Efik sentries to an adjoining trading post. Perhaps it was making dubious use of the Mission's privileged position, but it earned her the admiration of the merchants and the gratitude of the Quas.

Mary's rough-and-ready way of living, with its risks to life and health, troubled her colleagues, for illness and death stalked the Mission as usual. Mr. Anderson was gravely ill in 1881. In the same year Mrs. Sutherland, then Mrs. Anderson, died, mourned by the men-of-the-river who had been made to feel "less strangers in a strange land" by the kindness of these two formidable women.

Meanwhile an upheaval of another sort convulsed the Mission. Alexander Ross accused William Anderson, many years his senior, of adopting a too-tolerant attitude towards the unconverted. Violent ructions ensued which split the Duke Town Church from top to bottom. One of the Mission Deputies sent out to settle the dispute died victim to the climate. In the end Mr. Ross was requested to resign but instead set up an independent church hard by the existing one, causing the ordinary people to inquire if there were now two Gods in Calabar.

One can imagine the unsettling effect of all this on a small claustrophobic community. More than ever the young missionaries wanted to reserve their energies for what they regarded as the *real* struggle to bring light into the darkness of the country beyond— vexed by a situation of which one of them, James Luke, wrote

". . . as each new worker arrived, he was absorbed at the base, played out, and sent home or fell; and the passing days were marked by new graves in old ground with no attack developing."

The Deputies reported favourably on Mary's "manifold labours" at Old Town. In view of her great influence over the people and her stated preference for working single-handed, they recommended that she be allowed to stay on, although it was customary for lady workers to be assigned in pairs.

Emboldened, perhaps, by this official sanction, Mary made further trips afield and early in 1883 accepted the invitation of a Chief Okon to visit Ibaka (now James Town) thirty miles to the west.

Her reduced style of living had not diminished Mary in the eyes of the good King Eyo. Hearing of her proposed journey, he insisted on sending her in one of his own huge trading canoes, with thirty-three paddlers, so that she might arrive at her destination "not as a nameless stranger to a strange people, but as a lady and our mother".

The canoes of the great houses were splendid conveyances, thirty to forty feet in length and four or five feet wide. Each carried several drummers who kept time for the paddlers with an intricate, never-ending beat, while the men themselves crooned soft, rhythmic chants.

There were delays. The departure was at twilight instead of dawn. But at last, as her people at Old Town milled nervously about on the shore counselling caution and vowing vengeance if she should come to harm, Mary settled down against the rice bags in the little palm-leaf shelter amidships and found places for no fewer than *four* house-children among the feet of the paddlers. If she was not encumbered by quantities of luggage she could hardly be said to travel light!

Ibaka lay in the Delta creeks, low and airless. The village was dependent on fishing, since wild elephants trampled the crops. Few of its people had ever seen a white person and all took full advantage of the fact that the chief's room, in which Mary was hospitably installed, had no door. For a fortnight her every move and gesture was watched by a curious throng who commented with loud astonishment on her looks, clothes, ways of eating, drinking and attending to the children — and rushed to her assistance if she seemed to need help.

Even Mary found the evenings, when courtesy demanded that the wives, oiled and fattened like those of all men of rank, should sit around her in as close proximity as possible, almost past endurance. Rats, mosquitoes, flies, cockroaches she was accustomed to within limits, but in the crowded conditions of the chief's compound goats and chickens, wandering freely, added to the discomfort. Crowds dogged her footsteps wherever she went. Yet she managed to hold services, treat the sick and give simple lessons in housecraft and hygiene.

It was no wonder she suffered a near-fatal bout of fever after a tornado swept the roof off her hut, and soaked her and the children, with all their belongings. From the Anderson home at Duke Town she had written that it was unpleasant to be sick "on strangers". Although the people of Ibaka were friendly and concerned, she could hardly have felt more alone. Yet she disdained to be anxious in God's care. "What is courage", she would say, "but faith conquering fear?" She dosed herself with quinine and made, as she would often do again, arrangements in case she should die.

She lived, however, to engage at Ibaka in her first vital battle against the tyranny of custom. Two of Okon's wives, girls of sixteen, had gone visiting in one of the men's yards, and were to be punished by a hundred lashes each, and possibly have their ears cut off as well. When Mary protested at the severity of this, Okon agreed to let her speak for the girls before the assembled elders.

Like Anna at the Court of Siam, Mary faced men whose power over their women was absolute. Simple and ignorant they might appear, and possessed of little but the cloth knotted round their waists, a matchet, a gun, a few goats, cows or slaves. But the power of life and death was theirs. As they squatted on their haunches or perched on empty gin cases ready to listen, Mary wondered what on earth to say.

She began, with great tact, by declaring that the girls had been heedless and deserved punishment, but as the men nodded complacently she rounded on them with a scathing attack on a marriage system which gave lively young girls like these to a chief who already had a house full of women. The obedience the husband demanded was not, she declared, worth having.

The elders were astounded by the presumption of this strange pale-skinned, pale-eyed guest, and murmured angrily among themselves that the old "fashions" were a good deal better than the new. But she was their guest and they agreed to reduce the number of stripes to ten.

Mary had pushed them as far as they would go. She prepared such opiates as she could for the girls, who ran to her screaming when the lashes had been given and salt rubbed in the stripes, hoping that the chief would not regret tempering justice with mercy.

The return journey to Old Town came near to catastrophe. Chief Okon and his "senior" wife accompanied their visitors; but no sooner had the travellers eaten their evening meal of yam, herbs and palm oil, carried aboard smoking from the fire, than a fierce storm blew up and nearly capsized the great craft. There was momentary panic until Mary sharply ordered the paddlers to pull in to the bank and grip the overhanging branches.

The children buried their faces in Mary's lap while the lightning crackled and the rain beat down. As swiftly as it had started, however, the storm was over, Mary led her motley following in a quavering Efik hymn of thanksgiving as they resumed their journey, but, the crisis past, began to shudder uncontrollably with a malarial ague. The chief and his stout wife crowded close to warm her—for once she could be grateful for the customary blubber—and urged the paddlers to greater effort. Old Town was reached, its Mother safely returned. But, sick as she was, there were children to be dried, comforted and put to rest before she could find sleep.

The last storms of the rainy season wrought havoc that year and so damaged the Old Town house that Mary took refuge with the merchant whose beach adjoined hers until she could return to the comparative amenities of Duke Town. It was a disheartening time altogether. In February 1883, forty-nine-year-old Samuel Edgerley, an ardent explorer whose vision and practical gifts had held great promise for the extension of work up-river, died after a fall from his hammock while on tour. Mary herself became so sick she was scarcely expected to recover. She was invalided home in April.

4

A ROPE OF SAND

MARY HAD TO be carried aboard ship from her sick-bed, but she must have believed she would recover, for she took to England with her a tiny twin child called Atim Eso.

The baby was six months old. She had been found by a young Scottish trader who heard her crying in the bush. Somehow Mary located the slave-mother, who was very ill, and the other twin, a boy, and harboured them in her compound. The babies' father contributed a yam and one chicken to their upkeep and was seen no more. Five weeks later the mother was responsible for the death of the boy-twin, after which Mary kept the little girl by her night and day or she, too, would certainly have been killed.

So it came about that the career of one of Calabar's unsung heroines, faithful, indispensable, courageous Janie, began with a trip to Scotland. In Wishart church, Dundee, she was christened Janie Annan Slessor, after Mary's youngest sister, and in months to come she melted the hearts of congregations up and down the country.

Missionaries on leave were exceedingly popular as speakers with a mainly God-fearing, stay-at-home public. As soon as Mary was strong enough to address meetings, she was sought after from all sides. The contrast between her small stature and bold spirit made an irresistible appeal, though speaking was often a "torture". Leopard and crocodile, fevers, tornadoes and all the intangible terrors of the bush were apparently as nothing to her compared with the sight of a pious assemblage waiting to be addressed. Yet speak she did, and her appearances brought in considerable gifts of money. Janie, whom none of her own people would approach or touch, created a sensation everywhere.

So great was the demand for a sight of the two of them that the Foreign Mission Committee decided not to send Mary back to Old Town early in 1884, when she declared herself fit, but to capitalise on the interest she aroused by sending her off on a further round of lectures. Her views were clear and practical, expressed with pun-

The house at Ekenge
King Eyo's canoe

With Janie in 1883

gency, humour and a directness to which the simplest person could respond.

She believed strongly in the magnetism of personal touch and example. Out of one class of girls who heard her speak, no fewer than six eventually took up work in Calabar. But she longed to get back to her flock at Old Town. In December 1884 she was given leave to return, but asked to fill a vacancy at Creek Town, which she accepted only after hesitation.

Family problems then arose to make any departure impossible. Her sister, Janie, always consumptive, became so ill it was thought that nothing but a change of climate would save her life. But where should Mary send her? The journey to New Zealand had failed to save their brother John. Torn between her sense of obligation to the Mission, from which she had been so long absent, and passionate concern for her sister, Mary came up with a bizarre solution: she would carry Janie from the chill mists of Scotland into the dazzling sunlight of Calabar — in short, use the White Man's Grave as a health resort!

In her desperate quandary Mary persuaded herself that the notion was feasible. She wrote to the Foreign Mission Committee agreeing to go to Creek Town on condition that she be allowed to take her sister with her and build at her own expense a small mud house for the two of them. Given the prevailing view of Calabar, it was like asking to take an ancient grandmother on a foray down the Amazon.

Mr. Buchanan, the committee's secretary, gently tried to prepare her for the Board's reaction. Was Calabar really the place for one with a weak chest? How would Mary carry on her work should her sister react unfavourably to the climate or be obliged to return home?

The refusal of her application was a foregone conclusion, but Mary did not agree that it was in her own best interest, for now she had no alternative but to declare she could not return to Africa. It was a devastating blow to her hopes and dreams.

Nor was her sister's problem solved until an English visitor to Dundee suggested that the invalid might benefit from the milder air of Devonshire. Prompt in action as always, Mary swept her off to the south in February 1885, and quickly found a small house to rent at Topsham, near Exeter. It was Number 48, The Strand, one of a pleasant pair of Georgian cottages in that lovely riverside street.

The lawn behind the house went down to the River Exe and several of the windows gave views of the peaceful estuary. Spring came early and the air was pure and free from smoke.

4

Their mother soon joined them. The little family with the frail sister and black two-year-old, both named Janie, stirred a kindly interest in the small community. They made friends in the Congregational Church which they joined in April.

In no time Mary was holding Bible classes and addressing meetings. Villagers who seldom ventured beyond Exeter listened spellbound to tales of Old Town, Qua and Akim, of fatting house and Egbo runner and yam festival, of the "smelling out" of witches and of the twin taboo of which small Janie was so miraculous and smiling a survival.

But, that year, one blow followed swiftly on another. In May they heard with disbelieving shock of the sudden death of Susan Slessor. She had dropped dead on arriving for a visit with Mary's dearest friend in Edinburgh, Mrs. M'Crindle.

Since February Mary had declined to accept any further salary from the Mission, in view of her own uncertainty. Susan, therefore, had become the sole support of the family. Abruptly it appeared that Mary's earnings were more needed than her sustaining presence. Three months had worked an encouraging change in her sister's condition, and Topsham friends stood ready to help if help were needed. Mary therefore applied at once for reinstatement, offering to leave for Africa as soon as requested.

Her mother gave strong backing to this anxious decision. She had a favourite saying: "If one duty jostles another, one is not a duty." As she was convinced God intended Mary for the special work of Calabar, home obligations must not detain her.

But discussion as to where Mary was to be used dragged on through the summer and into the autumn, owing to the slow communications with Calabar. She appears to have spent some of this time attending the Exeter Infirmary to pick up what knowledge she could for her dispensary work. Of home nursing she had constant practice. Even the baby was sick that summer.

In October she learned that she was posted to Creek Town, but no sooner was her passage from Plymouth booked for the 11th November, than her mother, whose body was less stout than her spirit, fell ill with bronchitis. Then her sister suffered a relapse. Full of sympathy, the Mission Secretary proposed she should again delay sailing, but Mary could not reconcile herself to any further postponement. In desperation she wrote to an old friend in Dundee, begging her to come and take charge of the household until the two patients had recovered. Only the ready assent of this woman enabled her to sail as planned.

On the 4th December, after nearly three years' absence, Mary and little Janie Annan were welcomed back to Creek Town. To begin with, they lived with the Goldies, of whom Mary was very fond. But soon, as other missionaries went on furlough and all the women's work revolved upon her, Mary moved into a pleasant new "upstairs" house — and came closer to living in "civilised" state than she would ever do again.

She was soon back in her usual strenuous stride. Before long she had acquired a household of five children, most of them placed with her for training. The oldest girl, thirteen-year-old Inyang, ran the house, while three-year-old Janie made most of the mischief.

Janie was still, where Creek Town was concerned, that mysterious abomination, a twin. Her mother had died in their absence and Mary believed the child to be an orphan. One day, however, a man turned up at the mission house who declared himself to be Janie's father. He intended, with due caution, to satisfy his curiosity by glimpsing the child from a distance, but Mary laughed his fears to scorn. "Hoots, what harm can a wee girlie do you!" she cried, dragging him along to where Janie was playing and forcing him to submit to a hug. The man, emerging unscathed from the encounter, could scarcely bear to part with her and Janie received regular visits and gifts from him until he died.

This little girl, more at home with the coaxing accents of Scotland than with her native Efik, had grown very dear to Mary's heart, a link with the mother and sister who were so anxiously on Mary's mind.

Mails took four or five weeks and the home news did not improve. Mary tried to shorten the distance of separation with long, fond letters, making no effort to suppress the aching warmth of her love for them both.

[Your letter] brought you all so clearly before me. At church I sat beside the King and cried quietly into my wrap all evening.

Sad news was not long in coming. On the last day of 1885 Mrs. Slessor died of bronchitis at the age of sixty-four, and three months later Janie, a frail slip of a girl of twenty-four, was laid beside their mother in Topsham cemetery.

Within a year Mary had lost the last three members of the family she had been "caring and planning and living for" as long as she could remember. From being overwhelmed with responsibilities, she was left with none. "There is no one to write and tell all my stories and troubles and nonsense to," she grieved. "Heaven is now nearer to me than Britain, and no one will be anxious about me if I go up-country."

Her posting inland was, in fact, under discussion and there may have been a connection between the two events. Next to the consolation of religion, in the puritan ethos, came that of hard work. Purposeful toil was the cure-all for pain. In that close, kindly circle of which Mary was a part, given a proud, stubborn woman desolated by loss, there may well have been voices raised to say "Let her go forward as she so longs to do. It will take her mind off her sorrows." And to any who declared it too risky may have come the retort, "Is it likely, coming from such a family, Miss Slessor will make old bones?"

There were moves at this time to strengthen the up-river stations. Owing to commercial and consular pressures, the isolation of the inland tribes was coming to an end and the Mission preferred, where possible, to lead the way and prepare the people for changes to come, believing that the quality of that first approach was of prime importance.

It seemed both desirable and inevitable at this time that British administration should increase its grip on the Niger Delta, for several of the major European powers were displaying increased interest in Africa. The Berlin Conference of 1885 had acknowledged British spheres of influence along the Niger Delta. But a tremor went through the Calabar Mission in 1887 as the Germans, who had taken control of the Cameroons, forcibly turned out the Baptist missionaries there and took over their houses and schools.

At thirty-seven, Mary had ten years' service to the Mission behind her, half of that time in the field, and had from the beginning been dedicated to the idea of expansion. It was surely time to set her feet in the tracks of David Livingstone. Her chosen field was Okoyong.

It would appear from conflicting accounts that there had been a long-standing request from Okoyong for a teacher but also much opposition to receiving one. Mr. Edgerley had been seized and held for ransom there. A Calabar teacher who had been brave enough to attempt starting a school had barely escaped being murdered. The Okoyongs had a long history of bickering warfare with Calabar, and frequently attacked up-river travellers and interfered with trade. To settle a lone woman in such a place, therefore, required long and careful preparation.

The Okoyongs were, in a sense, outsiders, a Bantu-speaking tribe who had emigrated from the Rio del Rey into the hinterland of Creek Town, driving a group known as the Odot over the Cross

River in the process. They had little truck with the surrounding people except for meagre trading contacts. These had, however, sufficed to make Efik, the *lingua franca* of the Cross and Calabar Rivers, generally understood among them.

In 1868 several of the Calabar towns had waged more or less victorious war on Okoyong. But the outcome seems to have been indecisive owing to moral qualms felt by Christians in the invading force. When Okoyong offered to mark its surrender by burying a man alive, his tormented spirit to guard the treaty of submission from future breach, this tidy solution did not commend itself to the enlightened leaders of Creek Town.

Okoyong remained untamed. Its people and those of Calabar met only to trade in gin, guns and chains. Its scattered households, hardly big enough to be called villages, possessed no focal centre of power. They were, as David Livingstone had described the Bechuana tribes, "a rope of sand, no cohesion anywhere", "each independent of every other, distrusting one another". They lived, linked by little other than their own common xenophobia, in a perpetual state of feud.

> Each head of a house [wrote Mr. Goldie] with his people occupies his own locality in the forest and seldom visits his neighbour. When he does pay a visit, he is accompanied by a number of armed followers, and friendly intercourse among the people has yet to be created. They are always apprehensive that the power of witchcraft or charm may be employed against them, and it is only on the occasion of the saturnalia indulged in on the death or funeral rites of someone of consequence that they gather together. All the customs of blood which have been abandoned by Calabar prevail amongst them.

From December 1886 Mary and several other missionaries began to investigate the lay of the land and enter into negotiations with the chiefs. Mary wrote:

> Our first visits were not particularly cheering. Everybody seemed afraid to meet us, and when we did get them gathered, they and their followers were armed to the teeth. They offered to give a piece of land, and took us about that we might choose it; but they promised little else of a definite character, and indeed it was not until our fourth visit was paid—and I paid it alone—that they seemed to have any faith at all in our promises . . . Though each

visit found them less reserved and more friendly, the Chiefs *as a body* did not appear very enthusiastic . . .

For this last trip King Eyo, who had both a humanitarian and a commercial interest in seeing the Okoyong amend their ways, provided Mary with a canoe. Mary was more frightened than she would admit. But, seeing her come *alone*, the people thronged about her, calling her "mother". Chief Edem of Ekenge, the principal village, was sober, though his neighbour a few miles away at Ifako was not. Mary spent an instructive evening in Edem's compound, improving her acquaintance with his sister, Ma Eme, who was to become her staunchest friend. Her night in the women's quarters was serene despite certain difficulties.

> I am not very particular about my bed nowadays [she told a friend later] but as I lay on a few dirty sticks laid across and across and covered with a litter of dirty cornshells, with plenty of rats and insects, three women and an infant three days old alongside, and over a dozen goats and sheep and cows and countless dogs outside, you won't wonder that I slept little! But I had such a comfortable quiet night in my own heart!

Next day both Edem and the Ifako chief, now relatively coherent, agreed to give her land for her work. It would be, like the Mission land at Calabar, sacrosanct, a refuge for those charged with witchcraft or liable to be killed for any cause. This concession was vital. Mary later estimated that it had saved several hundred lives a year.

This visit confirmed Mary's belief that women, disarming suspicion, could be useful forerunners of the Church. She took a liking to the intractable Okoyongs as she had to the trouble-makers of Dundee, sensing the fear that underlay their bravado. She described them as conservative, independent, brave, *almost* fierce, war-loving and reckless. They were, she said, tall and muscular, with nose higher, mouth and chin firmer, eye more fearless and piercing, and with houses and habits much superior to the negroes of the coast. "Surely they will make good soldiers of Christ when they have learned to love Him."

Photographs do not bear out this euphoric description, but perhaps her own success on this occasion had bathed the people in a rosy light.

Nearly a year and a half after Mary's move was agreed upon by the Calabar Committee, final assent was received from Edinburgh with the grant of fifty pounds towards a house for her. Her way was clear to go.

The services of King Eyo's canoes were requested to transfer Mary, her household, and all her belongings, to Ekenge. The date was fixed for 4th August, twelve years but for a day after her first embarkation for Africa.

5

OKOYONG

WHEN THE GREAT morning came, Mary hustled her household early to the waterside, with their boxes, cases and baskets. It was raining, that endless, heavy-dropping rain of the tropics that softens at times into a steaming mist only to pelt down again, rattling on tin roofs and seeping through thatch. A gloomy setting for the start of a brave but very doubtful venture.

When King Eyo's canoe arrived—late—the crewmen gave trouble over the loading. Against a background of noisy argument the Creek Town people, Mary's flock, gathered mournfully, full of dire forebodings on her account. She herself had deep misgivings—not because she feared for her own life, but because she knew what extraordinary strength of will would be necessary if she was to make any headway among the people.

Her trader friends freely delivered themselves of the opinion that the only thing that would change the Okoyongs was a gunboat. Many of her Mission colleagues doubted if it was the job for a woman. Mr. Goldie, however, stood by his opinion that the people were well-disposed towards her.

This was the moment Mary had lived through in fantasy as a small child, and had worked and prayed for, for twelve long years. But as the delays mounted her nerve threatened to desert her. It took her friend King Eyo, who arrived towards noon and sorted out his canoe men, to calm her fears. Much interested in this undertaking, he promised to keep in touch with her by his fleet of trading canoes and to send help if needed.

Mary and five children, aged between one and eleven, took their places amidships in the palm-roofed "cabin". But suddenly Mr. Goldie could not bear the sight of the little troupe setting off unaccompanied. He called for a volunteer from the Mission staff to see them to their destination, and John Bishop, the printer, agreed to go with them. The people on shore waved and wept, the man at the stern began to beat his drum, and the heavily-loaded dugout pushed off into blinding rain, in the direction of the Calabar River.

It was near dark when the canoe drew up on the beach four miles distant from the village of Ekenge, which was to be her head-quarters. Mary was counting on the people to serve as carriers, so, while the printer supervised the unloading, she went on ahead with the children and the most essential stores. She intended to contact her hosts and round up some men to fetch the loads, while she found her quarters, made a fire, and got the children fed and put to sleep.

The eldest boy led the way through the forest, balancing the "chop" box which contained their bread, tea and sugar on his head. Two smaller ones, frightened of the dark and weeping, followed with the cooking utensils. Janie trotted after, also in tears, while Mary, with baby Annie astride her hip, brought up the rear. The rain poured down. All of them were soaked and shivering. Night fell, which it did suddenly in that latitude, and they had no lantern to scare off any lurking leopard. Mary sang foolish songs to divert the children as they stumbled forward.

The coming of the "white ma" would have been no everyday event in such a place, and ordinarily news travelled with uncanny swiftness. But an ominous silence hung over the approach to the village. No one came out to meet them, and when they reached it, Ekenge was dark and deserted. Only two slaves could be found in the chief's compound. These informed Mary that the people had all gone off to Ifako, two miles beyond, to the funeral feast of the head man's mother, and would not return for four or five days.

One of the slaves found Mary an empty hut in the women's yard, helped her to make a fire, and brought a calabash full of water. The other hurried off to inform Chief Edem of her arrival. The hut was in a filthy state, but nothing could be done just then. While the kettle boiled for a meal of bread and tea, Mary stripped off the children's wet clothing, dried them as best she could, and tried to comfort their fears. When they had eaten she settled them to sleep on the bare mud floor, huddled together to warm each other, for there were neither sleeping mats nor dry garments for them until the boxes came.

At the riverside, Mr. Bishop waited in vain for carriers, then tried to persuade the canoe men to help him up to the village with some of the things. But the men were worn out with the long haul from Calabar and refused. He set off himself to see what had become of the promised helpers and, fetching up in the village without having met a soul, found Mary, still in her wet clothes, keeping watch in her doorless hut over the sleeping children.

There was nothing for it but to round up the few slaves left guarding the scattered farms on the edge of the village and go back to the waterside. Mary went barefoot, for she had taken off her sodden boots and her feet were now too swollen to fit back into them.

All was silence when they reached the river. The men had rolled themselves up in their loincloths and were fast asleep in the canoe. But Mary could not wait for morning. Not even in these circumstances would she have her possessions humped about on a Sunday! She waded into the water and, shaking the men awake, insisted with a mixture of threats and good-natured ragging, that enough of her loads be got up to the village that night to see her through until Monday. Having brought them grumbling to their feet, she distributed the essential cases and baskets to be loaded on to their heads and they disappeared in darkness. At last Mary followed. It was early morning when she stretched her worn and weary limbs across the stacked-up boxes — there being no space in which to contrive a bed — and fell thankfully asleep. How John Bishop spent his night has not come down to us, but it was certainly in damp discomfort. New to the country, he had none of Mary's mastery of the language or the situation. But she was grateful for his presence: "Had Mr. Bishop not come with us, I don't know what I would have done . . ."

The "miserable, wet, idle Sabbath" that followed must have come near to being the low point of Mary's life. Committed to a future of inconceivable hardship and difficulty, alone except for five querulous, frightened children, her strength played out, she faced an empty village, indifferent to her arrival, and was powerless to complain. She had put herself beyond the rule of law. No treaties bound the chiefs of Okoyong to respect life, not even hers. In all the wild, wedge-shaped country that surrounded her there was no outpost of trade or officialdom where she might seek companionship or comfort, nor any other missionary.

The rain poured down. The hut was so stacked with cases there was scarcely room for movement. The walk through the night had left them all with scratches and bites that irritated and threatened to fester in their squalid surroundings. The merest flicker of interest from the "lost ones" she had come to save would have made all the difference to Mary, and when a few women appeared, having come back to the village for food, she spoke eagerly to them of the promise of the Christian life. But she had to tread warily until Chief Edem returned.

Fortunately the dominating passion of Mary's life was the breaking of new ground. As she squatted in the damp hut, neglected by her hosts, cooped up with stray hens, rats and complaining children, with packing cases for furniture, and for light a cotton rag guttering in a dish of palm oil, she could at least exult that she was free to live and work as she alone saw fit. Free, too, of the burden of trying to live her life on two levels. No ship's officer would happen in in expectation of those delicate refined touches for which the Mission ladies were renowned, no reproving colleague delay her as she dashed from one call to another with "Out without your hat again, Miss Slessor?" As in those comfortless days when most of her family possessions were in the hands of the pawnbroker, and destitution hung over them, Mary's spirit burned bright.

Meanwhile, practical considerations saved her from despair, for there was a family of six to provide for. Though she had brought ample provisions of staples like flour, sugar, tea, tinned milk and soap, fresh food had to be obtained from the market, which was some distance away and held only at intervals. In later years she could write with humour of "the cares of housekeeping where there is no baker supply, no butcher supply, no water supply, no gas supply, no coal supply, no laundry supply, no trained-servant supply, nor untrained for that matter, except some native can and will lend you a slave to help you or when you can buy one . . ."

That first Sunday she had not even a habitable hut nor any friend among the people.

On the Monday and Tuesday the remainder of her possessions were brought up from the beach. Mr. Bishop fitted a door and windows they had brought with them into appropriate holes in the wall of the hut. Then he was gone, and Mary left "alone with mud and rain, gaps round doors and windows, rain pouring on boxes and bedding".

By midweek the people began to filter back into the village, but a quarrel arose and they traipsed off to indulge in another week of rioting in which five men died. Mary, by her own account, spent this time "mudding, cutting bush and felling trees to get a few necessary conveniences". First among these must surely have been a wash room and latrine for her personal use, though she forebore to say so. She fenced in a portion of the yard to reserve it for her washing and cooking, rigged up curtains to give her a minimal privacy, and made a partition of packing cases to provide a modesty barrier for when the boys and girls lay down at night to sleep. Since some of the cases had to be moved out of the hut each night to make room for the family to sleep, much of each day, when the sun shone, would be spent drying out their contents. Fortunately the dry season was not far off.

Yet this time of hiatus had certain compensations. For when the people returned, Mary, lodged in the heart of the women's quarters, became the object of incessant, uninhibited curiosity. Not only was she herself a non-stop entertainment; so were the unaccustomed objects with which she was surrounded—her clock, her chest-of-drawers, her meat safe. She could not even be alone to read her Bible or say her prayers. Sometimes she picked up a matchet and, going out into the patch of land assigned for her use, hacked away at the undergrowth so as to escape company and commune with her Lord.

Finding the people "not insensible to kindness", she accepted all this with wry good humour. But the incessant bickering of the women's quarters, the unjust abuse of slaves—the scoldings, floggings and sometimes mutilation to which they were subject—were almost intolerable. Even the children, many of whom, being slaves, had to live by what they could filch, were "such a pest to everyone that it is almost impossible to love them". Yet the terrible punishments inflicted on them, by starvation or branding, made her rush to their rescue. She declared that only her sure sense of the nearness of God saved her from losing her reason in a situation where she was daily witness to such cruelties, and where the drinking, drumming, and dancing sometimes kept her night after night without sleep.

For, she wrote, "*everybody* drinks". The drink traffic "baffled" her pen. "I have seen four shillings' worth of lawful trade done with Calabar, and I have seen barrels of rum and boxes of gin by the score every week." Even the children were primed with spirits, as a dog or duck might be, to give amusement with their drunken antics.

One day she found a crowd gathered and discovered that an eleven-year-old boy who had run errands for her when most of his fellows were at the burial feast, was being subjected to the ordeal by boiling oil. At first she didn't realise what was happening—not until she saw the scalding fluid dipped from the cauldron and ladled over the boy's hands and he fell writhing and screaming to the ground. His extreme pain was satisfactory evidence to his accusers of his guilt. But what had he *done*? asked Mary. They told her he had deserted the "old fashions" and she understood that it was his service to her that was meant. Furious, she grabbed the ladle and rushed at the man who had used it, vowing she would test *his* innocence in the same manner, but to the hilarious amusement of the crowd, he dodged her efforts. For once, there was nothing she could do.

It is surprising there are not more accounts of victimisation of Mary's adherents, for all over the area there was fierce opposition to change. Six young men at Unwana were sentenced to death for *wearing clothes*. When an African Mission agent protested at such drastic action, the people first agreed to sell the men into slavery, then were persuaded to accept a fine. But the men's houses and possessions were destroyed.

Possibly Mary's excellent knowledge of all that went on and her determination to see justice done would have made such victimisation profitless. Nothing so set her apart from the usual run of hardworking, self-denying missionaries as her constant, *active* intervention at the scene of any trouble, which gave pause, at the very least, to her opponents.

Even this was not always a success. Once she interceded for a slave who had been accused of sorcery and condemned to death. Her interference was angrily resented by a milling throng, armed with guns and matchets; but Mary refused to leave the accused man's side. A curious paralysis of will afflicted the people when she chose to stand her ground in this way. Whether it was the strangeness of this white woman or her invincibly cheerful assurance and apparent imperviousness to fear, they were unable to carry out sentence of death in her presence. Moreover, they lacked her tenacity. On this occasion the excitement simmered down, the man's captors wearied and his life was spared.

But it was a sad sort of victory. Instead of being poisoned or beheaded on the spot, the slave was chained to a stake in the very yard where Mary lived, flogged daily, and left to starve. There was only a mud wall and rough door between her and the scene of these prolonged torments. Her protestations had no further effect. He was unconscious and all but flayed alive before his accusers finally unchained him.

Chief Edem and his widowed sister, Ma Eme, were, however, not without concern for Mary's well-being. Ma Eme had herself survived an ordeal which gave her some sympathy for the victims of customary law. Head wife of an important chief, she and his other wives had, on her husband's death, been seized and held suspect as was usual. A white fowl was beheaded at the feet of each wife in turn and according to the way it fluttered in its death throes, each woman declared innocent or guilty. In such cases the "guilty" often had their arms and legs broken and were thrown alive into the husband's grave, so that it was little wonder that, large and strong as she was, Ma Eme fainted dead away when the verdict was pronounced in her favour.

She had not long returned to her brother's compound, with this experience fresh in her mind, when Mary came on the scene. From the first, while outwardly adhering to all the traditional ways, she gave covert assistance to the white woman whenever the saving of life was concerned.

Mary's presence created awkward problems for the chief. He had expectations, no doubt, of those material and social benefits that generally followed in the wake of the white man. But the flouting of his authority, however tactfully attempted, cannot have been easy to bear. And, as news of the white woman spread, there were unwelcome visitors. One band of drunken women hoped to wheedle spirits out of this reputedly well-to-do member of their sex. Edem, her protector while she lived under his roof, himself stood guard all night at her door to prevent them breaking in. When morning came they got nothing from the fabled "white ma" but a severe dressing down in their own language, and left invoking angry curses upon her.

Notwithstanding all this, by the end of her first month in Okoyong, Mary had opened a school in the chief's yard. For two weeks she wrote, *everybody* came. "Bond and free, male and female, old and young, all crowded into the shed. The master and his sister, who can claim a pedigree few can claim in this land, are hustled by slaves bought but yesterday." Singing "of the simplest kind" provided a great attraction. Many soon mastered the Efik A.B.C.

When the novelty wore off, the school settled down to about thirty pupils. It was often interrupted, however, by rival demands on Mary's time. She would not brush aside any call for help in favour of school routine, believing deeply in "the daily mixing with the people" as a prelude to change, and welcoming their demands upon her.

This attitude made possible her lone-handed approach to a seemingly impossible task. The people came first. The catechism could wait. Her first aim was, in the words of a friend, "to uplift the people and make human life safe".

The attentions Mary received from the chief and his sister unfortunately did not extend to speeding on the erection of her house. Both Ekenge and Ifako had agreed to put up buildings for Mission use but it had been no surprise to her, on arrival, to find nothing done in either place. She began to wear the chiefs down with almost daily reminders, but month followed month without a start being made.

Near the end of the year she wrote, in excuse for not extending the scope of her work to outlying farms:

> ... It will be truest economy to husband my strength for the house-building. I am entering on the fourth year of my term, so am not so strong as I was 3 years ago, and am living in a single apartment with mud floor, and that not in the best condition. Moreover it is shared by three boys, and two girls, and we are crowded on every side by men, women, goats, dogs, fowls, cows, rats and cats, all coming and going indiscriminately, so there is no accommodation for being sick, and it is too far to go to Calabar to lie down ...

When neither complaint nor pleading produced any result, Mary began to clear the ground herself, not only to acquire more space and privacy for her household, but to establish Mission rights to the land so it could become a place of sanctuary. She burnt down brush and hacked out roots until at last one day, seeing their white mother so strangely engaged in work they would in time have felt moved to do for her, her people concluded that the building season had arrived and turned out in a body to begin.

Mary worked with them, designing, as it grew, a two-room hut of mud-and-wattle which could serve as kitchen and outbuildings when the larger mission house was built. Meanwhile she could fence in and occupy her ground and oversee the work as it advanced.

Each room was roughly eleven feet by six, with a pounded mud floor and palm-leaf roof which extended in front to make a verandah. Store rooms jutted forward at each end.

As her furniture was scanty and her family large, Mary contrived some built-in fitments of solid clay—a bunk, a seat beside the cooking fire, and even a sort of sideboard. The whole was pounded and polished until it was as dark and smooth as mahogany. The room thus equipped served as the general living room. The one beyond held most of Mary's belongings, her books and boxes and sewing machine, her little folding organ and her bed. Anything that would hang, from cooking pots to reading charts, was slung from the bamboo rafters, within and without. Mary called it a "caravan", but it had real doors and windows with glass panes, and seemed to the villagers "fine pass all".

Her fame spread. She had treated one of Edem's wives, bitten by her husband in an access of drunken affection, and had successfully

averted blood-poisoning. Hearing of this, the chief men of neighbouring villages began to call on her, urging her to visit them, and
eager enough for her favour to lay down their weapons before
crossing her threshold.

One day the chiefs of Ifako summoned her to see the start they
had made on a building which was to be both church and school. To
her astonishment she found that the ground had been cleared, the
materials stood ready, and she had only to mark out on the ground
with a stick the dimensions of the structure that would become the
first Christian church in Okoyong.

Not a single slave was employed in its erection. Mary had
insisted on this. King Eyo sent up the roof mats from Creek Town
and the chiefs' own wives and daughters carried them the six miles
from the waterside. They also "mudded" the walls. Included in the
plan were two rooms at the end for Mary's own use when she wished
to stay overnight, rooms which had, she wrote with satisfaction,
"every convenience they know of".

The dedication of this building was a popular occasion and passed
off with "none of the levity which generally characterises the introduction of any novelty", and with every child "radiant in some sort
of garment".

Even in the 1880s the missionaries' passion for clothing the
people, often in wildly incongruous raiment, seemed to many people
unnecessary and absurd. Consul Johnston spoke approvingly of the
Baptist Church in the Cameroons where young women attended
church quite modestly without a stitch of clothing. Mary was
remarkably free of the prudery of her generation, but she maintained that the wearing of a garment never failed to create self-
respect, no mean point considering that the Mission adherents were
often people totally lacking in status. She was pleased, on successive
Sundays, to see the clothes kept in their pristine state. If dress was
the *only* mark of the churchgoer, it did at least evince a willingness to
entertain new modes of life and to shake off the profound conservatism of the tribe.

Her own meagre possessions created a furore. She was not averse
to stimulating the people's desire for shirts and curtains if this dis-
tracted them from their preoccupation with feuds and drink.
"Everything I have they declare they must get," she wrote. "The
clock, and the organ and the sewing machine . . ." Before her own
machine became useless with rust, she cut out and stitched up
countless editions of the simple smock which had become something
of a uniform among the churchwomen of Calabar.

In her report to the *Record* on her first months in Okoyong (from which the quotations in this chapter are taken), it is clear that she felt the overcoming of suspicion to have been her main achievement. The people had started to build their houses as close to hers as possible. They were bringing her their disputes to settle, in small matters, and in large ones seemed ready to approach King Eyo for arbitration. She described instances of chiefs visiting chiefs where drink had been "put aside" at her request and the guests departed "in soberness and peace, a great wonder in this place".

She may have feared that such vague social improvements would be considered unsatisfactory by Scottish parishioners who put their hard-earned pennies in mission boxes and made bundles of cast-off knickerbockers in the expectation that these would bring sudden light out of darkness. How to explain, for instance, that her most valued friend, Ma Eme, remained resolutely "heathen", her name never to be added to the tally of converts which was the home Church's clearest measure of the success or failure of its overseas work.

Yet the secret support Ma Eme gave Mary in the battle for the weak and oppressed against powerful chiefs and elders was undoubtedly of more value than a public confession of faith. For, seeing her sacrifice regularly to her household gods, the menfolk did not suspect that it was to the chief's sister that the white Ma owed her uncanny foreknowledge of events.

Traditionally there is a strong bond among women in the Calabar region which has made them at times a potent political force. It may have been this sense of sisterhood that the shrewd, motherly African felt for the hard-pressed Scotswoman by whose teachings she was never wholly convinced.

Mary tried to explain that "results" were hardly to be expected. As she saw it, "Faith cannot exist without knowledge, and they have hardly as yet got over the very first principles. Their minds are almost a blank in regard to spiritual things and their superstitions make them fearful in regard to anything new to them ... The harvest *will* be gathered, but as yet it is only the seed time ..."

6

WITCHCRAFT

FEW NINETEENTH-CENTURY missionaries made much study of the religious beliefs of Africans or even granted them the name of religion. The untutored state of the native African, his irrational terrors and unscientific remedies, seemed to render worthless any consideration of his philosophy. "Superstition", "idolatry", "devil worship" were what the newcomers saw around them — an evil contagion to be avoided and destroyed at any cost.

This was the era when Christianity, enlightenment and progress were devoutly believed to be as one. The progression through paganism and witchcraft to general acceptance of Christian ideals that had been the pattern in Europe, would, it was expected, be repeated in Asia and Africa, the missionary's task being to hasten this inexorable process. If the missionaries considered themselves and their ways "higher" than the Africans and theirs, it was in the same way as they considered their generation in advance of all those preceding — all mankind, as it were, being placed somewhere on the staircase to glory.

Having no anthropologists to interpret for them, the missionaries had little idea of the strength of the forces ranged against them. As Dr. Ajayi explains it, the "traditional religion was an attitude of mind, a way of explaining the world, a way of life. It was expressed in laws and customs hallowed by time and myth as being essential for the well-being not just of the individual, but of the community."

No one in our generation needs to be reminded that the missionaries were often short-sighted or narrow minded, their attitudes repressive, joyless and grim. One traveller finding on the Duke Town school blackboard the words, "They that do evil shall go down into hell", felt little surprised at the poor attendance. Missionaries were frequently unable to distinguish between the harmful and the harmless in native culture. Because the masked Egbo men were known to perpetrate outrages on women, the missionaries found it hard to reconcile themselves to any of the vivid and eloquent "plays", masquerades, and dances which were the people's main cultural outlet.

But most of them believed strongly in the potentialities of their primitive parishioners, though *not* in their innocent virtue. To people who exalted the life of the "noble savage" in her hearing, Mary would retort: "Let them go spend a month in a West African harem!" She was not belittling the Okoyong when she wrote, "We are a different race from them, and while they know that our God and our knowledge is far higher than theirs, they think they need not aspire to that as they are so far inferior to us . . ." She believed that they had only to grasp at the spiritual truths she offered to shake off that inferiority—even that, by God's grace and goodness, they might do so at once.

By any standards the Okoyong people were in need of help. Caught between their own punitive hereditary customs and the protectionist policies of the coastal chiefs, they seemed doomed to extinction. In her evidence before a Royal Commission inquiring into the liquor trade twenty-odd years later, Mary declared that the people were "utterly besotted" and "visibly dying out", through drinking and fighting, and that when she first went among them it was impossible to settle disputes "because they were all drunk before we began". Mary Kingsley found that human sacrifice and the administration of the poison ordeal, even for the pettiest crimes, were decimating the population: ". . . thus over immense tracts of country the death rate exceeds the birth rate. Indeed some of the smaller tribes have thus been almost wiped out."

Surrounded by unnecessary suffering, Mary could do little more than tackle each problem as it came. But she sensed that contact with the people at the deepest level of their existence was better achieved by allowing herself to be borne along the mainstream of their lives than by setting up model institutions.

Everything Mary did demonstrated the value she placed on life. She nursed the orphaned babies of slaves, normally discarded as being no one's responsibility. If their lives could not be saved, she buried them with simple ceremony. Milk crates were coffin enough for such small corpses. The naked crowds watched incredulous as Mary dressed the tiny bodies in hand-sewn nightgowns, or whatever the mission box afforded, only to lay them beneath the ground. Yet the importance that these acts lent to even the most transient spark of human life was not lost on the onlookers. Often there was just one person—an aged grandmother perhaps—who was touchingly greatful for the love it showed.

She taught in much the simple way she had herself been instructed, with the alphabet and numbers, Bible stories, prayers and catechism. But as her fame as healer and peacemaker spread out along the bush paths, from one market to the next, she was increasingly called upon to act in the public interest. More often than not, her opponent was the intangible, overpowering force of witchcraft.

In a village near the Cross River some eight hours' walk from Ekenge, a chief lay dying. The dread of the ritual killing that was sure to follow lay over everyone, but especially over the women, slave and free. Once they would simply have waited — helpless, fatalistic — or fled to the bush. But on this occasion there was a woman among them who came from a village near Ekenge, whose grandchild had been cured of illness by the "white ma". At her suggestion four brass rods (representing about a shilling in the local currency) and a bottle of gin were sent off by messenger to Chief Edem, beseeching Mary's help.

The chief and Ma Eme opposed her going. Their protection was good for only a short distance. What would happen to her in the bloodletting that would take place if the sick man died? The rains were still at their peak, all paths blocked by floods, the forest one great swamp. But for Mary a call was a call.

Edem, however, delayed her departure by ordering the messengers to fetch an escort for her. Mary spent a sleepless night. The country where she proposed to go was a closed book. She was well aware that in risking her own life she put the whole project at Okoyong in jeopardy; it would be almost impossible to find a replacement for her. Mr. Goldie believed that her influence over the Okoyongs was hers alone and could not be passed on — a contention she derided but could not ignore.

Her mind was made up for her at morning light by the arrival of a female bodyguard — the men having prudently avoided trouble by remaining outside Ekenge. Mary kissed her children, commended them to the care of God, and set forth. It was her first trek into wholly uncharted country and she could not help wondering how much truth there was in the horrific tales each village told of the next, or what she might find on arrival.

She set off, all decorum, in dress, hat, boots and stockings, the everyday wear of a woman of her times, and carrying an umbrella against the pouring rain. One by one, as these became soaked, clay-sodden and too heavy to bear, she stripped them off and deposited them in the calabash of one of her escorting amazons. The umbrella broke and was tossed into the bush. But even in her petticoat she was over-dressed for this expedition. Its clinging wet skirts wrapped themselves around her ankles, and it soon went the way of the rest. Mary marched on in her calico chemise.

The chemise of those days was a decent garment, as modest as the modern "shift", high at the neck and reaching to the knees. Mary came to prefer it for this kind of travel, but it would have been highly unconventional in European company. She was startled when the path opened suddenly into a crowded "palaver-ground" and she had to run the gamut of hundreds of eyes before finding herself again on a narrow bush track. One lot of villagers tried to turn her back, but she brushed their threats aside and continued without further interference to her destination.

The village, when they reached it, was armed and waiting for the worst. Mary, after her soaking, was shuddering violently with a malarial chill. While her own clothes dried over a cooking fire, she donned an unappetising assortment of garments provided by the women, and immediately went to examine her patient.

The nature of the chief's malady is not on record, but Mary decided other medicines were required than those she had brought with her. Knowing the direction of the path they had taken, she asked how far it was to Ikorofiong, a mission station on the other side of the river, where Alexander Cruickshank had a well-stocked dispensary. Could anyone go, she asked?

There was the usual outcry at the suggestion that anyone should risk his skin by crossing to a village of strangers. There *was* a track to the river, and a canoe *could* cross, but they would be killed if they went. At last a Calabar trader, whose mother was of the sick chief's village, but who nevertheless lived uneasily in his canoe at the riverside rather than chance its hospitality, was persuaded to go for them.

Mr. Cruickshank, at the tidy mission station where he had lived for seven years and would stay for forty-seven more, probably shook his head when he received Mary's message, at the thought of her getting into such a predicament without essential supplies. It was as well he was spared a sight of her in her underwear! He and his wife, however, made up a bundle with the medicines she had asked for, an encouraging note, and a few small comforts like tea and sugar. Brewing up the tea in a borrowed basin, Mary took courage.

In the morning the chief's condition had much improved. It would be puzzling to guess how an amateur in medicine, called to what was assumed to be a deathbed, could work so remarkable a cure in so short a time, unless the trouble was something as simple as constipation which a heavy dose of Epsom salts would cure. But, where illness and accident are assumed to be the result of malignant forces at work, fear plays a vital part in sickness. Here the substitution of a brisk, cheerful woman, apparently immune to witchcraft, for the native doctor intent only on identifying the witches, might well give the patient a new lease on life.

Mary lingered for a day to reassure herself about her patient's progress and to satisfy her own curiosity about this unfamiliar locality. The people seemed eager to learn. She promised to send them a teacher and to make trading contacts for them with the outside world, delighted to realise that the bugbear of the hostile enemy hordes was destroyed. She could go where she liked, in and beyond Okoyong, without grave hindrance.

A similar incident occurred in Ekenge. Chief Edem fell ill with a severe abscess on his back and Mary began, as a matter of course, to care for him. But she arrived in the chief's hut one morning to find a rival healer in attendance. A chicken lay impaled on a stick and various charms were tied about her patient. Edem pointed out that his cure depended on the detection and punishment of those who had bewitched him and "willed" his sickness. When Mary scoffed at this, he swore that he had "proof" in the form of a collection of teeth, bones, shot and seed which the native doctor had drawn out of his back. These were displayed to her. Then, feeling he had fully justified himself, Edem ordered a number of his people to be chained up pending punishment.

Mary was determined that "her" chief of all others should not shed innocent blood if she could prevent it, but, forbidden by Edem to interfere, could only pray, through many days of strain, for his recovery. The celebration that then followed was as rough and riotous as any Mary had known, but all the hostages were freed except (as the chief put it) for "one worthless slave woman". Mary believed she had been sold as a sacrifice.

Most of the misery Mary found was a result of belief in witchcraft. Inanimate signs and objects could inspire overpowering dread and have consequences measured in terms of life and death. Such apparently unreal situations were a sore trial to a commonsense Scotswoman. It was useless to belittle these fears. She could only stand firm in her own courage and faith in the midst of them.

A blustering, trigger-happy chief came to visit Edem, whose women were, with good reason, apprehensive. Mary kept a stern Presbyterian eye on their visitor through days of feasting. At the first intimation that he was thinking of home, she rounded up his followers, who were brandishing guns and matchets and getting beyond control, and managed to steer them all onto their homeward path. She even went with them to prevent trouble in other villages along the way — villages that were often little more than an extended polygamous household and easily at the mercy of a troupe of armed men.

She was jollying them along with some success when they suddenly halted abruptly at sight of a plantain sucker, coconut shell and palm fruit arranged in symbolic fashion on the path. This was very strong *juju*.

Reading instant menace into the objects, shaking with fear and rage, the men turned about to wreak vengeance on the last village they had passed through, supposing the people there to have placed the *juju* in their path. Mary had to act quickly. Almost without thinking she began running. She was swift on her feet and, unlike the rest of them, perfectly sober. She circled past them until she was out in front and could turn and face them all, a thin white figure, arms akimbo. Incredible as it seems, the men stopped dead in their tracks. They shouted and argued. She remained immovable. At last, thwarted and confused, they allowed themselves to be marched once more towards their home village.

But there in the path lay the *juju*. With a laugh, Mary picked up the fruit, handling it to demonstrate its harmlessness, and threw it aside. But none of her party would cross the spot where it had lain. They skirted the area in a wide arc and in doing so evidently obtained more liquor, for they rejoined her more unruly and quarrelsome than before. Mary lost all patience, and with the help of such of the group as were responsible, tied up the worst miscreants and secured them to trees. Then she escorted the remainder home.

Seeing them delivered, Mary hurried back towards Ekenge, releasing her surly but now quiescent captives as she went. When she reached the scene of all the excitement, she picked up the plantain sucker and took it home.

But the power of the *juju* was not broken. Convinced that witchcraft was being used against him, the chief sent to Mary next day, demanding the plantain sucker.

Poor Mary knew — for Chief Edem told her — that the sucker would mean death to someone and tried hard to avoid surrendering it. But she was forced to hand it over.

The chief proceeded to make the suspected villagers prove their innocence by taking oaths in the presence of the plantain sucker.

Although no particular victim was indicated, the blood of a man was demanded, and a young man carried off and chained.

Now Mary was forced to go and plead for the prisoner. The chief, possibly to punish her for her high-handed behaviour of the day before, laughed in her face, then stalked off to his farm, the classic means of escape for the polygamous husband when cornered by stubborn women. Humiliating as it was, Mary followed, knowing persistence to be her best weapon.

And so it proved. In a few days, without reason, the young man was released unharmed. In true African fashion, everything fizzled out and was forgotten.

This bizarre story contains elements with which she was to be constantly confronted: the irrational fear inspired by an outwardly innocent object, the rounding up of suspects by the witch doctor whose task it was to "smell out" the persons who had cast the spell, the manipulation of evidence in order to pay off scores, leading to the slaughter of victims who might well be innocent. It was nearly impossible to bring such palavers to an end because of the fresh feuds to which each incident gave rise.

It is clear that much of her work had to do with breaking the stranglehold of fear in which the people lived—fear of death, of witchcraft, of evil spirits, of twins, of ghosts of ancestors, of poisoned food, of the *accusation* of sorcery. These were not lightly to be argued away. For though the missionary might scorn the powers the people held in dread, or demonstrate that she was not harmed by them, what was *she*? Perhaps a witch herself, or at least a being apart, and not susceptible to the same ills and dangers as themselves.

But fear of strangers and of the world outside Okoyong was, Mary felt, a fear that might reasonably be overcome. She determined to divert the attention of the Okoyongs from their petty wars and witch hunts to the joys of trade. It was David Livingstone's belief, and hers, that traffic in men and spirits could only be stamped out by the demands of legitimate commerce.

When Mary suggested that Okoyong might trade with Calabar, Chief Edem declared, with a grin, "We do so, Ma, we trade in heads." She sent to Calabar asking that someone should bring up a selection of the common articles of trade: cloth, soap, basins, needles and thread, mirrors and the rest. But no one dared to come.

Okoyong is a very dark tribe [she wrote]. They are the princes of drunkards, and smash and hash at each other and all and sundry as none of the other tribes do. Calabar people are so frightened of them that to ask any one to come to see us is to bring a volley of *isungi* (abuse) or *imam* (laughter) down on your head. They would as soon think of going to the moon as of going to Okoyong . . .

She continued, however, to whet the curiosity of the local chiefs with stories of Calabar life and of the houses and dignity of the great chiefs, particularly the wise King Eyo. To Eyo she suggested that a palaver be arranged with Okoyong to settle some outstanding disputes. He responded promptly by inviting Okoyong's leaders to Creek Town.

All the nearby chiefs agreed to join Mary in this expedition. A canoe was loaded with farm produce of yams and plantains, palm kernels and palm oil, in the most respectable country fashion. The Okoyong were not boatmen, however, and the canoe promptly sank. Another canoe was found and loaded with greater discretion, and at last came the momentous departure. Several travellers got cold feet at this point, and several more changed their minds when it became clear that Mary refused to allow them to carry arms. "Things were at a deadlock," wrote Jesse Hogg.

Ma spoke plain words about keeping promises, but at first they positively refused to leave their arms behind. "Oh, Ma, you want to make women of us. Of a truth you want to make women of us!"

She made as if to go homeward, and after a battle royal with some of them down on their knees holding her feet, and all talking and expostulating at once, they gave in. The weapons were transferred to the women and slaves, but with some reluctance. Something suspicious about the cargo caught the vigilant "Ma's" eye as she stepped into the canoe, and on inspection she found contraband in the shape of swords! These swords were flung out with a good many epithets as to the general untrustworthiness of the Okoyong people. At last they paddled off, and she did not keep a "tied-up" (Calabar expression) face for long, but only long enough to be good for them!

King Eyo proved himself a tactful statesman. He dealt patiently and courteously with these crude country cousins who were traditional enemies of Calabar, and constrained his brethren to do the same. His respect for Mary and deference to her Christian God so impressed the men of Okoyong that they were induced not only to accept his ruling against them in the current dispute but to agree to his arbitration in the future. Unarmed as they were, the men of Okoyong returned home with unimpaired dignity and much to tell.

Arrangements were made for the future sale of produce to traders in Creek Town. In the wild oil palm, Okoyong possessed a ready source of wealth which had so far been tapped only for home use. Now all this was to change. Okoyong had opened its door a small crack.

7

ORDEAL AND SACRIFICE

AS A RESULT of the Calabar jaunt, Mary's stock with the Okoyong soared rapidly. The story of the great visit became known in every hut. The returned travellers impressed on their fellows how the rich Christian king with his fine house, countless slaves and numerous trading canoes, welcomed their "mother" as a friend and equal, deferred to her judgment and stood ready to grant her every request. Her own people thought perhaps they had been deficient in their attentions and, hearing of the rivalry among the Creek Town chiefs in erecting splendid houses, saw a way of indicating their revised assessment of her importance. Mary was scarcely awake the morning after their return when she heard sounds of activity in her compound, and found that one of the chiefs had turned out a working party to begin building the mission house for which she had so long been clamouring in vain.

Mary planned it in the style of the mission houses of Calabar, though it was to be built of local materials. Store rooms—also useful for housing refugees—would be on the ground floor, while her own rooms above opened on to a broad verandah, to catch what occasional breeze stirred. The "caravan" was now to become kitchen and dispensary. In their current mood the chiefs determined she should have no less than the best, and the framework of poles lashed together with palm-fibre "tie-tie" was tall and strong.

Meanwhile, in Scotland, a cheery, practical handyman named Charles Ovens, who had knocked about the world a bit, had the matter of Mary Slessor's house brought to his attention. An old lady of his acquaintance, having read Mary's first report from Okoyong in the March 1889 *Record*, suggested, "I see Miss Slessor wants a man to put in her doors and windows—why don't you go to Calabar?"

Capable artisans for the mission field being scarce, Charles Ovens had no sooner offered himself, than he was appointed and sped on his way. In July he arrived at Ekenge with Tom, his African assistant, and some dressed timber.

To Mary, alone and unhoused after almost a year, no visitor

could possibly have been more welcome. He was a man of her own sort, straightforward, good-humoured and used to living rough. He spoke with her own rich accent, had a loud infectious laugh, and sang, as he worked, all the old Scots songs. He could turn a hand to anything, baby-minding included.

He found the lady his old friend held in such high esteem sitting barefoot at her dinner in an open yard full of goats and chickens. Her new house, however, had reached the stage of having its palm-leaf roof put on. Mary showed it to him with inordinate pleasure and pride.

Charles Ovens was the first of her countrymen to see Mary in action in an emergency. In August, a year after her arrival in Okoyong, he and Tom were getting on with the carpentry work on one of those peaceful, sunny workaday mornings that made Ekenge, occupied with its hoeing, seem more a tropical Arcadia than the seat of iniquity it was usually painted, when an anguished cry from the bush disturbed the quiet.

Without a moment's hesitation, Mary dashed off in the direction from which it had come and found the chief's son, Etim, lying unconscious in the middle of a clearing where he had been building himself a house. It was plain that the case was serious. A heavy log had slipped and fallen on the young man and he was paralysed. Ovens, who had followed her, helped improvise a stretcher out of his shirt and a couple of bamboo roofing poles, and together they got the lad back to his father's house. But the carpenter was at a loss to understand Mary's tragic look or the quaking terror of the bystanders.

Mary enlightened him. An accident of this kind was never attributed to natural causes. And if a young man of Etim's standing died, the killing of suspects for sorcery was sure to follow. When a chief had died a few years earlier, sixteen slaves, twenty children and four wives had been sacrificed.

For the next two weeks Mary nursed the sick youth day and night and, as it became clear that he was not to be saved, racked her brains for a way to stave off bloodshed. Hearing the sound of wailing one morning, she rushed to find Etim insensible while a last effort was made by all around him to recall his spirit. Pepper was being rubbed into his eyes and forced up his nose. His mouth was propped open with a stick. The shredded fibres of a palm-nut were set alight to send smoke up his nose. All the household, particularly his uncle, Chief Ekpenyong, were yelling their loudest to guide the spirit back to where it belonged, but life was gone.

The witch-finder was summoned, examined the omens, and declared a nearby village to be responsible for Etim's untimely death. A party of armed men at once went off to raid the village for hostages and returned with a dozen men and women, whom they chained up in the yard.

Mary knew by now that these things happened out of a deep-ingrained sense of what was necessary—out of what one writer on witchcraft calls the "tragic fallacy" that, for its believers, points a convincing connection between one cause and another effect. But killing for the dead had a dual purpose—punishment for the instigators of the sorcery and the provision of a retinue in the spirit world. With the intention of making Etim's onward passage so splendid that he could dispense with followers, Mary set about bedecking the young man's corpse in the most extravagant conceivable fashion.

To the European suit she had given his father she added yards of silk. On his painted head she placed a plumed hat and put rings on his fingers. When the corpse had been seated in an armchair in the women's yard, a large umbrella, symbol of a chief's rank, was stood over him and a silver handled whip placed in his hand. A mirror was placed so that his ghost might enjoy the overall effect. There were, Mr. Ovens wrote:

> . . . more than two dozen women sitting singing him on his way to the other world. The yelling seems to me like fiends. Then there are about fifty men armed with swords and guns. There are twelve people in chains, three mothers with infants, and some young men brought from the next village. If Miss Slessor or I leave they will all be put to death.

So far the people approved Mary's actions and she had kept a place for herself in the inner yard where nothing could happen without her knowledge. She proposed, with Ovens's help, to stand guard over the prisoners every moment until the burial had taken place.

She assumed the night duty. For several nights she sat out the hours of dancing and drumming and drinking while the prisoners slumped in their chains and filth, and more and more barrels of rum were rolled in. The carpenter wanted to get his tools and cut the prisoners free when no one was looking. But Mary had learned that no precipitate act was so effective in these affairs as unrelenting, inexhaustible patience. She sent him off to make the most elaborate coffin he could.

Just how the prisoners were to meet their fate was not clear until they saw preparations being made for the poison ordeal.

> We saw them begin to grind the bean [wrote Ovens]. Miss Slessor told them we would not allow them to do as they proposed. By this time they were nearly all drunk and running about with their guns loaded and swords in their hands. However, they did not frighten us.

The relatives of the dead man became furiously angry at Mary's interference, but were incapable as ever of carrying through the poison ordeal while she was present. They unchained one woman and led her away into the inner yard where the corpse sat enthroned, placing Mary in a fearful dilemma. She hardly dared leave the eleven remaining prisoners, yet instinct told her the woman's danger was greatest.

At last she darted into the inner courtyard just as the woman was presented with the poison cup. Seeing her lift it to her lips Mary hissed, "Run!", grabbed her by the hand, and the two of them slipped out of the compound before the men recovered from their surprise. Together they sprinted for the sanctuary of the Mission compound where Mary thrust the woman through the door, with a shouted word to Ovens to hide her, then raced back to resume guard over the others.

The harried chiefs now tried to talk Mary round. The ordeal, they claimed, as usual, would only harm the guilty. Mary, as usual, disputed this. But flies were beginning to gather round the corpse. Burial could not be postponed indefinitely. They agreed to let two of the prisoners off with the *mbiam* oath.

The ingredients of the *mbiam* drink were not of themselves deadly, though the dread in which it was held might make it so. Hope Waddell compared it to the "bitter waters" of the Hebrews, which would destroy false swearers. In the version Mary Kingsley cites, the oath took the form of a long litany disclaiming all evil intent and climaxed by "Then, Mbiam! Thou deal with me." It was the ultimate in solemn vows, enough to satisfy the family mourners.

The two men took the oath and went free. At Mary's entreaties, five more were allowed to do so. This, to the minds of the chiefs, left the guilt resting squarely on the man and two women who remained and they swore they should never be spared. Mary did not abandon hope, however, or leave the scene.

Another day went by. Mary was threatened with the power of

Egbo, even with the burning of her house, but *no one laid a finger on her*. Chief Edem railed and raged, but Mary stood her ground. Time went on, with much milling about and nothing decisive happening, as it does in Africa. At last Ma Eme intervened to get one of the women with her baby released into Mary's care. She was so loaded with chains there was no fear of her going far. But the feeling against her was so strong that Mary barricaded the gates of her compound to keep her safe. A large packing case became her cell.

Mary had one astounding trump card still up her sleeve. She had sent off a message to Creek Town requesting what was to be the final embellishment to the obsequies of the chief's son. And now, in answer to her call, there arrived two missionaries who proceeded to set up their equipment and give a magic lantern show! There had never been anything like it in Okoyong and it created a sensation. The night that followed was quiet. The missionaries departed and Mary went back to the job of haunting Edem's tracks.

To the perplexed father, angry and incredulous by turns, harrowed by the conviction that he was failing to do right by his dead heir, Mary's insistence seemed insane. He nevertheless handed over to her the last male prisoner, certain she would be satisfied to allow one insignificant woman to "drink doctor". The woman herself was by now begging for an end to her misery.

Mary was not appeased but, as the urgent preparations for the young man's interment went forward, she doubted if she could do more. She put her own children to bed that night unable to rid her mind of the thought of that wretched woman, expecting any moment to hear that it was all over with her. But suddenly there was a weak voice at the barricade, and, outside, a half-dead creature crawling in chains. She claimed she had broken her own manacles to escape, but Mary always believed that it was done, not by her, but by Ma Eme.

Only a cow, the umbrella, looking-glass and other splendid accoutrements, plus the glorious memory of that magic lantern show, went down into the grave with Etim. Not a human life was taken. Such a thing had never been known before in Okoyong.

But bloodshed was not wholly avoided. In the drunken excitement at least one man was killed and others injured. A party of Egbo runners arrived to avenge the death of Etim and dozens of women took refuge in Mary's compound. Though there was much shouting and popping off of guns, they passed through Ekenge without incident, but went on to lay waste the village named in the original indictment for witchcraft. It was several weeks before the women Mary had rescued could leave the shelter of her household.

Furthermore, a new rumour that Chief Ekpenyong, uncle of Etim, was the person *really* responsible for his death led to a fresh sequence of events. Mary now had strong adherents among the women who warned her that Ekpenyong intended to free himself of suspicion by taking the poison bean. Mary pestered him into promising he would do no such thing, but a secret search of his hut brought eleven beans to light. She took them away but, hearing a commotion behind her, turned back and found the chief drunkenly struggling with his women for possession of a bag which he swore contained cartridges and palm nuts. Mary demanded to see its contents and, to the anger of his henchmen, impounded forty more beans.

Ekpenyong left the village, resolved to die like a man and in peace. Mary pursued him several miles to the house of a neighbouring chief. Here the feeling was not so inflamed as in Ekenge and Mary's good-natured mockery made her so much the obvious winner that she found she had plentiful support. No one would support Ekpenyong in his determination to take the ordeal and he compromised by swearing his innocence on *mbiam*. Shame nevertheless prevented his return to Ekenge and he removed himself and all his family to another part of the bush.

One further incident in these violent weeks illustrates yet another facet of traditional "justice": When the eldest son of a chief fought and beheaded one of the guests at Etim's funeral, general warfare seemed sure to follow. Mary succeeded in getting the parties to take the matter to a chief at Ikunetu, by the Cross River, for arbitration. But on his correctly declaring the chief's son guilty and death the penalty, the family attempted to settle the matter by substitution, first of a slave, then of a small brother and then—when these were not accepted— by a twenty-year-old brother. Custom accepted the forfeit of one life for another to pay off scores, but Mary did not. She rejoiced to hear that the brother had escaped to the other side of the river. He was shortly caught and strangled, however, satisfying the offended parties but leaving the murderer to go free.

There still remained the problem of the village burnt in reprisal for Etim's death. Crops and stock had been destroyed and the people who had escaped dared not return. Mary persuaded Chief Edem to show mercy. Under relentless pressure from her, he even added the offer of fresh land and seed for planting. It was a noble gesture. The hamlet slowly came back to life, its people strong adherents of the

"white ma", and Edem himself seemed thankful for a peaceful outcome to the whole shattering upheaval. He even went so far as to
admit that he and his people were weary of many of the old customs.

At last Charles Ovens could get on and finish the Mission house.
The Ifako church was given doors and windows and, as his last
project, the carpenter put a door and padlock to Mary's hut at the
riverside. Mr. Goldie had sent her a canoe, since many journeys were
easier by water than by land, and Ma Eme's people had made her a
small hut to keep it in, where she could sleep if benighted.

They were now installed in comparative luxury in the new house,
but the carpenter had scarcely occupied the guest bedroom before he
went down with malaria. Mary nursed him until he was well enough
to travel, and missed his company and conversation badly when he
returned to Calabar in September.

Full of wonder at what he had experienced in her company,
Charles Ovens wrote to the *Record* describing the events of his time
in Okoyong. As Mary's own reports tended to stress the routine side
of her work, this may have been the first time that her friends
appreciated the full scope of her efforts or the extent of her pertina-
city in time of trouble. Killing for the dead had been suppressed in
Calabar by the concerted protests of missionaries, traders and consul, implemented by trade boycotts and, at times, gunboats, but
usually *after* the deed was done. It is to be doubted if any of Mary's
forerunners was so determined to forestall *any* preventable taking
of life as to sit out without fear or wavering such a time of turmoil
as he described.

The sense that something extraordinary was developing in
Okoyong out of Mary's deep involvement with the people stirred the
hearts of the faithful in Scotland. Mr. Ovens told how he had seen
her push men over, grabbing them by the neck and throwing them
to the ground, to stop them getting at the rum that wrought such
havoc among them. She had pulled a loaded gun out of the hands of
a drunken visitor and kept it a whole week on her own verandah,
defying him to try to recover it. Ovens had seen her smack full-
grown men as if they were obstinate children, for refusing to drink
the medicine she prescribed. And she had brought an end to one
dangerous fracas by going in among the men and simply *demanding*
that they lay their weapons down on either side of her. When they
had done so, she stood between two stacks of guns and matchets
that were nearly as tall as herself. She looked on these episodes as her
daily job.

Even the old-timers in Calabar were astounded by what they

6

heard from Ovens, and no little amused by the effect Mary had produced on the plain carpenter. But that autumn there was a new-comer in Duke Town who could not hear enough of the gallant, single-handed struggle being waged in Okoyong.

Charles Morrison, a twenty-four-year-old schoolmaster from Kirkintilloch, had arrived in the country not long after Ovens. His father, a successful bootmaker, had been deeply identified with home Mission work, which had given the studious son a strong grounding in Christian work and the desire, in spite of indifferent health, to serve overseas. Something of a poet, his imagination was deeply stirred by Ovens's tales of the interior. He himself was struggling with the difficult Efik language, with its tonal variations and dialect changes, and was keenly conscious of the disadvantage of having to teach in English. What sort of woman was it who could enter into the very heart of that African life and thought from which he felt himself so cut off? He was soon to find out.

During 1890 Mary was often ill, in spite of the amenities of her new house and the privacy it gave her. Occasionally she visited Calabar for rest and recuperation. She had been more than four years on the coast, under continuous pressure and strain. Although Mr. Ovens swore he never saw a frown on her face, he certainly saw her at times in the grip of malarial fever, that most depressing of ailments. Generally she threw it off quickly and with little break in her activities, but less easily as the years went by.

Now she felt able to leave Okoyong to its own devices for a few days at a time. Her medicine, she wrote, "and the fact that God has blessed it in some instances marvellously, has made the whole country mine. Every chief, more or less, has been under my care, or some of his people have been, and they have expressed in various ways their appreciation of my services. No white person need fear to go anywhere now."

The children went with her to the town. If the missionaries on whom she descended without warning, followed by her numerous brood, were sometimes assailed by inhospitable qualms, they had no need to be, for Miss Slessor's wants were few and both she and the children were quite comfortable sleeping on the floor.

Charles Morrison met her on one of these occasions when her stay was lengthened by illness. He discovered in her a reader as avid and discerning as himself, sensitive in her judgments and possessing a lively critical mind. To talk of books and ideas was for her a rare luxury. For him there was a charming incongruity in the soft voice and roguish humour of this legendary woman of action before whom strong men quailed—a woman childishly gay and tender with her bairns. Probably he never felt the sharp edge of her tongue, which was reserved for the pompous and obstinate. Their friendship grew and he accepted her invitation to come—now that she had a proper house and guest room—and see for himself the real Africa behind the coast.

Mary reached a point where she was seldom without fever and her need for home-leave was painfully evident. But she would not hear of leaving her station until she had been relieved. Mr. Goldie was certain no African agent would be tolerated by the Okoyong people and doubted the ability of any European to fill Mary's shoes. But a recent arrival, Miss Dunlop, had the courage to volunteer and the advantage of some training in dispensary work. She was sent up to get into the way of the place, and her first impressions were favourable.

The house was besieged with people who had heard of Mary's impending departure and, in the cordial way of the bush, wished to make their formal farewells and leave parting gifts. But there was no respite for Mary. Shortly before she was to go, at the year's end, a palaver arose which threatened to break into full-scale war. She was advised not to try to intervene, as her ship was due in Calabar, but she could not leave her people on the verge of bloodshed.

It took her most of one night, following false trails and wilfully misled by the frightened people, to track down the opposing factions, who were heavily armed and keyed for action. Normally her greatest protection was her utter defencelessness, but in this inflammatory situation she enlisted an Egbo drummer to march before, drumming to warn the warriors of her approach. Arrived, she prowled the no-man's-land between the hidden forces in the threatening silence, unable even to meet the combatants face to face, but determined to treat with both sides before action began. At last a friendly face emerged sheepishly from the undergrowth and turned out to be that of a chief whose life she had saved.

This was the break she needed. With his help, negotiations for peace could begin. Mary, however, knowing her men, demanded food first. "I am not going to starve while you fight, and meanwhile you can find a comfortable seat in the bush where I can confer with the two sides; choose two or three men of address and good judgment for the purpose."

Hours of litigation followed. Mary had had only an hour's sleep, but sat it out to the end, patiently interpreting one side to the other, prodding them towards agreement, until a settlement was reached.

She was then alarmed to see that the agreed payment was made in cases of gin. There was little doubt but that the hard-won reconciliation would dissolve in alcohol the moment her back was turned.

With the excitement at a climax, it was useless to speak or shout, and Mary was half-dead with exhaustion. As the cases were produced and the bottles taken out, she tore off her dress and petticoat and threw them over the stack. The men pulled back in uncertainty. Mary had honorary status in the Egbo Society — to have touched her garments would have been to violate a protected person. There was wild uproar but no one touched the gin. Mary cornered the only available tumbler and doled it out, a drink for each man of influence. Then she dismissed them to their villages, promising to send the remaining bottles after them.

This was achieved after extended wrangling. Moreover, the parties to the quarrel swore to keep peace during her absence from Okoyong and she felt certain they would do so. She slept that night in a village hut, but with a quiet mind. Next day she hurried back to Ekenge to find that her baggage had already been taken down to a launch which awaited her at the riverside.

She was sick and worn out. But a momentous decision was reached before she sailed from Calabar. Charles Morrison, Mary's junior by eighteen years, proposed marriage. Mary consented on the clear understanding that they should work together at Okoyong.

No correspondence survives to tell us what components of love or sympathy, mutual idealism or practical enthusiasm entered into this unlikely contract. The partners to it were discreet. Mary sailed with copies of Boz and *Eugene Aram* inscribed in her suitor's hand, and her secret intact.

8

ROMANCE AND REALITY

ONCE AGAIN JANIE, now nearly ten, travelled home to Britain with the only mother she knew. It is not clear how many other children had to be farmed out during Mary's leave. Some, placed with her for schooling, had families to whom they could return. Others were reclaimed by relatives once they survived infancy and could look after themselves — a thing African children learn early.

But there were several whom Mary regarded particularly as her own and, for their safety, kept with her on her travels about the district. Four-year-old Annie was part of that inner circle as close to Mary as flesh and blood. The child of a slave-mother who had died of *mbiam* — that is, after swearing the dreaded oath — she would have been buried with her mother had Mary not intervened. Her father was alive, as was her mother's mistress. They took charge of her at times, and probably did so now. (On a later occasion, however, Mary discovered that the woman was trying to sell the slave-child, claiming she was "swollen" and could not return, after which visits to her Creek Town home discontinued.)

Janie, however, remained closest to Mary's heart. The child's earliest memories were of Britain. Like Mary, she thought of it as "home". She had spoken English (with a strong Dundee accent) as her first language, and sung the familiar Scottish songs and hymns from babyhood.

On landing at Plymouth, the two went straight to Topsham to renew friendships of five years earlier and visit the graves of Mary's mother and sister. They took a small house in the centre of the village, called "Majorfield", and through the spring and summer Mary gave herself up to the slow recovery of her health.

One wonders how much she dreamed, as her strength returned, of a future with Charles Morrison at her side. Time had taught her caution in the building of hopes, particularly amid the freakish fortunes of Africa, and Charles was not robust. She must also have realised that there were difficulties that could not be wished away. The only grounds on which she would contemplate marriage were that she and Charles should carry on her work at Okoyong together. On this she was adamant.

On the surface this sounded unobjectionable. Two missionaries doubling the work that could be undertaken, giving one another help and support, and living that exemplary life so uplifting to native populations, must surely be twice as good as one! Furthermore they intended (or Mary did) that they should go on leave at different times and so forever solve the staffing problem at Okoyong.

But Charles seems to have known this would not do. Exciting as was the challenge of the inland tribes, he was a highly-qualified teacher engaged in the all-important work of training future mission agents and ministers. There was as yet no formal school of any kind in Ekenge—only rudimentary classes carried on, in Mary's absence, by mission boys—while Duke Town was perennially short of teachers. It is hard to see what part a young man of mainly literary leanings could have been expected to play at Okoyong as it then was. He begged Mary to say that, if their proposed arrangement proved unacceptable to the Mission Board, she would join him in Calabar.

This she would not for a moment contemplate. She could not turn her back on all she had achieved at Okoyong. "My life was laid on His altar for that people long ago," she wrote to a friend, "and I would not not take one jot or tittle of it back."

Nor was the subject broached with undue haste. It was September before the couple's joint request was brought before the Board. But they must have felt some confidence in the result, for their engagement was made known to friends, and Mary, short-cropped as usual and looking considerably younger than her forty-two years, was photographed wearing her engagement ring.

Meanwhile, Mary left Topsham on the inevitable round of speaking engagements, more of a strain than ever after so many years cut off from her own people and language. She made a base with her old friend, Mrs. M'Crindle, in Joppa, near Edinburgh, but through June and July, and again in September and October, she had four or five engagements a week in different towns and was constantly on the move. A stay in Kirkintilloch enabled her to meet her fiancé's family.

On her previous leave she had urged special work with women and children. At Okoyong, however, she had been dismayed by the lack of fruitful, skilled occupation for men. Mere literacy could not improve the lot of the bush man as it might the citizen of a busy commercial seaport. Thinking ahead as always, she began to plead for the training of young Christians in manual skills.

In the forty-five years since the first King Eyo Honesty complained that he had "too much man now I can't sell slaves, and don't know what to do for them . . ." practical forms of missionary work had not been forgotten. But the Mission's teaching, aimed at propagating the Gospel and so based largely on the kind of education the missionaries had themselves received, had produced clerks and catechists, preachers and teachers, a white-collar élite. Craftsmen had still to be brought out from England or the West Indies.

Little investigation had yet been made into the adaptation of local products and materials to European use. European houses were imported whole, in prefabricated units, and their furnishings either imported or made on the spot by foreign artisans from imported raw materials. It was widely felt that neither the finished articles nor skill in making them would be of much use to Africans, who anyway might lack the necessary perseverance to complete their training.

James Luke, in Scotland recuperating from blackwater fever, believed with others that Calabar was not "ripe" for industrial training, and said so in a letter to the *Record* which called for more European artisans. In a masterly reply (January 1892) in the same magazine Mary seconded his call but urged that these men should be used to train future generations of skilled African workers, declaring her faith in the will and capability of the people to learn, and demolishing every previous argument against the notion.

> There is an idea abroad that our wood is unworkable. Would it be like God's ordinary way of working to make hundreds of miles of unworkable wood? A great part of our export is ebony. Our natives, with a sixpenny matchet, or an ordinary hatchet, make canoes, paddles, doors, tables, seats, bedsteads, sofas, etc. and the first Rev. Samuel Edgerley of our mission's history himself sawed native wood into flooring for his house . . . If we could teach the natives to manufacture . . . it would utilise the materials lying at our hands; it would elevate our people, and it would give a profit to the Church.

To add force to her suggestion she called out, as it were, over the heads of a Foreign Mission Board perennially short of funds, to the Church at large, presenting it, moreover, with a practical blueprint for action:

> . . . surely there are half a score of leisured men in the United Presbyterian Church who could make this matter their special business and could bring it to a practical issue. For instance, £200

would send a deputation of two, to see what the capabilities of the country really are; to examine the timber, the indigenous and possible products, the water power, the character and probable cost of building, etc. They could interview the Kings, Chiefs, and other natives of influence, finding from themselves how far such work would be appreciated and supported by them; and meanwhile their visit would be a help and pleasure to the Mission staff, a stimulus to native Christians and a blessing to the heathen outside . . .

As for the form the scheme should take, she had concrete proposals:

Each workman could manage his own department, live in his own compound with his own men, influence them, educate them, have stated days on which he will accompany them, either by boat or on foot, to the villages and hamlets all round—he thus learning the language and the manners of the people . . .

Mary's letter was both so sound and so tightly argued as to leave a well-meaning Church with no choice but to implement it. The Mission Board begged her to meet with them to discuss the matter further.

But Mary had retreated to Devon and was only with difficulty persuaded to return to Edinburgh. When she did so, before sailing from Liverpool in February, she appears to have carried the day.

She had not managed so well, however, where her private affairs were concerned. In November she and Charles Morrison received letters to the effect that since Mr. Morrison had expressly offered his services for Duke Town, the Board could not now sanction his move to Okoyong until "full provision" was made for carrying on the school. Assurances were given, however, that every effort would be made to secure additional teachers.

No mention in these of their projected marriage. And Mary was evidently unwilling to indulge in any special pleading on that account. The story goes that her reply to the Mission secretary was simply, "Poor Charlie! Pray for him." But as the year wore on with no wedding bells, and impatient friends began to ask whether she wouldn't, after all, reconsider joining Charles in Duke Town, Mary responded,

I could not leave my work for such a reason. To leave a field like Okoyong without a worker and go to one of ten or a dozen where the people have an open Bible and plenty of privilege! It is absurd. If God does not send him up here then he must do his work and I must do mine where we have been placed. If he does not come, I must ask the Committee to give me someone, for it is impossible for me to work the station alone.

Such reticence existed in the private affairs of people like these—*Miss* Slessor and *Mr.* Morrison even to their nearest associates—that we may be forgiven for indulging in speculation of a kind that has been avoided elsewhere.

Was, for instance, the engagement of a forty-two-year-old spinster to a newly-appointed stripling of twenty-four something of a scandal in the Mission? To the Africans, among whom men of standing chose to wife the very young and nubile, in hopes of plentiful progeny, the alliance would have appeared grotesque. But Charles's family in Kirkintilloch seem to have welcomed the match.

And what were Mary's feelings? Might she, heart-whole so far as is known until then, have, in the loneliness of middle age, been swept away by tender feelings so far as to forget that Charles was young enough to be her son? One can appreciate the appeal of the sweet-tempered, high-minded and frail young man to a woman of her intensely maternal nature. But there was little about her of the frustrated spinster. She had a houseful of "bairns", a full and exciting life, and overflowed with affection for the people around her. And marriage as she had known it in Dundee was no particularly enviable condition.

From Charles's point of view, Mary's personal magnetism was considerable. She had the gift of infusing young men with her own vitality and love of adventure. And—with her slight stature, lively sense of fun and vigorous unorthodoxy of behaviour—she probably seemed younger than mission ladies half her age.

But nothing seems to have mattered to Mary quite so much as the continuance of her work at Okoyong, and Charles was bound by his own strong Christian conviction to respect this. No one knows what he really felt. His passion for Mary may have equalled hers for Okoyong. It is a poignant thought and fits in well enough with his subsequent decline in health and disconsolate wanderings.

He was invalided home in May, when Mary wrote a moving letter to his mother saying that, since they were determined the Lord's work should not suffer, Charles and she must part; but should his health improve and the way be opened to them, their engagement would stand.

He never regained health sufficiently, however, to get permission to return to Calabar. He was advised to seek a dry climate and, when no suitable mission post could be offered, went off to join his brother John, who was working on the building of the great railway in North Carolina. There, in a hut in the woods, he busied himself with literary work until his death not long afterwards. The letter Mary wrote to his mother, when the news reached her, left his family in no doubt that the bond between them was heartfelt and strong.

If, on her return to Calabar at the beginning of 1892, Mary felt her resolve weakened by a reunion with her Charles, she also found herself more deeply committed than ever to the territory of Okoyong. For far-reaching changes were taking place. During the year she had been in Britain, her countrymen had established firmer control over the region now known as the Oil Rivers Protectorate.

Calabar was the headquarters of its new and admired Consul-General, Sir Claude Macdonald. Courts had been established in the settled areas and twelve vice-consuls appointed to administer the various districts. There was an army of three hundred soldiers in barracks in Calabar and a naval patrol boat, the *Beecroft*, to keep the waterways open. Customs, marine, postal and medical services were being established. Civilisation was finding a toe-hold.

The Consul-General called on Mary at Duke Town to learn what he could of Okoyong. Although the Protectorate was established in name and had considerable resources at its command, including the support of most of those powerful coastal chiefs interested in trade, its influence would only slowly permeate inland. It was dedicated to promoting freedom of trade and establishing a rule of law that would eliminate those "murderous practices" that had been worrying consuls since the days of Beecroft—by peaceful penetration where possible, but by the use of limited force where long and continued resistance was given.

Mary believed in the necessity for British control if conditions of peace and justice were to be brought about. But she told the Consul-General that the people at Okoyong were not ready to tolerate a government official in their midst, nor to accept without bloodshed the sudden introduction of new laws. She herself could mediate in their disputes because she was intimately acquainted with the language and people, but no stranger could do so as yet. Sir Claude then suggested that she might be empowered to hold court and transact necessary government business in the district.

Mary gave this proposal much thought and prayer. She was already overworked. The Calabar Presbytery were not eager to have their people identified with political authority, and she herself shrank from administering justice under the law. But there was the precedent created by David Livingstone thirty-five years earlier, when he accepted consulship on condition that he be considered first and foremost a missionary with freedom to act according to Christian conscience. And she had only to imagine to herself some raw young administrator arriving to settle Okoyong's palavers by the rule-book to see that she had little choice. She agreed to become the first Vice-Consul of Okoyong.

The changed situation in the coastal town, with its soldiers and officials and plans for building—there was even a Botanic Garden—was highly favourable to the kind of training scheme Mary had so recently advocated. Skilled labour was urgently required and the government were ready to help with finance. Already, as a result of Mary's prompting, the wheels were turning that would lead to the establishment of the Hope Waddell Training Institution, to teach tailoring, printing, carpentry and engineering, and profoundly influence a new generation.

Okoyong, however, had changed little in Mary's absence. Miss Dunlop had revised her first good opinion of the tribe, found she had little influence over them and declared herself glad to get away from people who came to church drunk and boasted of their "lawlessness". The usual sad fugitives—ill-used slaves, men and women fleeing from accusations of witchcraft—awaited Mary in the mission compound. Ma Eme was ready as ever to send warning of trouble, using their agreed signal—an empty bottle with a request for "ibok" (medicine) to alert Mary for whatever might break. Sometimes it was simply a quarrel which she could settle by exercise of patience, authority and a caustic tongue. Sometimes it was witchcraft, the poison ordeal, a case of a kidnapped child or slave. But it was not unusual for her to spend days and nights away on such an errand, sleeping by the intended victims wherever they might be, without opportunity to change her clothes or cook food. Sometimes she knitted furiously to while away the long hours and still her own fears till litigants grew weary and tempers cooled.

Between whiles there was the same heavy, humdrum labour day by day, as a letter to Dundee friends shows:

27 May, 1892

. . . You would hardly believe that it is so much work to repair a place. You are used to stone and lime, and boarding, but our mud and sand is very easily let out of order, and will not patch up. It has always to be renewed. I have not been washed and dressed till night time since I came out. But God has been very gracious to me. I have not had a single ache or pain beyond fatigue.

There was also a fair share of amusement and satisfaction. Of the visit of one of the mission carpenters who had gone up to help her, she commented:

... He said, as we sat at my beach one day, "What wd some of the braw folk of Edinburgh think if they saw you just now?" Referring to my bare feet and *very* unconventional dress. He sat on the ground as I did, so I just said, "What wd they think if they saw you?" A woollen undergarment and some unmentionables on his understandings, he looked as much a tinker as I did. He is the man for our place ... It is splendid to have people who knew your people at home, and who can sympathise with your inclination to shout "Hallelujah" sometimes ...

9

"THIS VERY WONDERFUL LADY"

THE WORLD BEGAN to find Mary out in her forest fastness. Consular messengers arrived at her gate with lists of court cases requiring settlement and travelled about with her as she held hearings on this chief's verandah and in that one's yard, maintaining a severe formality in the proceedings that made up for the lack of legal trappings. Though her judgments had more often the flavour of a maternal admonition than a judicial decision, they were duly recorded and returned to Calabar, and Okoyong gave the Administration little trouble.

Now that the river was patrolled, travel was somewhat safer and officials and missionaries dropped in on her more frequently. Mails arrived, about once in three weeks, with reasonable regularity. It was even possible, though still risky, to tramp unmolested down forest tracks to Creek Town, but Mary was probably alone among white people in doing this, on occasion, alone and by night.

Stories of the "White Ma", of her commonsense justice, ready wit, cool nerve and startling disregard for health or comfort, circulated among officials who were taking up posts in the inland area of the Protectorate. Exaggerated health-precautions were the rule with most Europeans (even into the middle of this present century) newcomers being warned not to touch so much as an unslippered toe to the bedroom floor (for fear of jiggers) nor lean out of an open window unhatted (for fear of sunstroke).

Pink-cheeked young administrators schooled to wear sun-helmets and mosquito boots, sleep under nets, and boil and filter their water, were staggered to find Mary striding hatless, barefoot and unarmed through districts they preferred to approach with a posse of police, unladen (except for the inevitable baby that would cry if put down) and unescorted. They saw her calm the wrath of men bristling with weapons with no more than a good-natured dressing down in the vernacular. And romantics among them, over a drink at the club in Calabar or Opobo, began to dub her the "White Queen of Okoyong".

Her work was back-breaking, and her consular duties added to the load. With schools and dispensaries to see to, a permanent houseful of children and women—often sick—and now visitors as well, the demands on her time were endless. The days when she could sit out a poison bean "palaver", or remain watchfully on the scene until a chief had been buried without human sacrifice, were coming to an end.

In 1894 she decided something must be done to stop killings which she herself could no longer effectively prevent. She was occupied in one village with a case of twin-murder when she heard that in another a slave was about to be given the poison ordeal. She sent a message to his accusers asking them to delay proceedings until she could be present; but a tornado delayed her departure and she found on arrival that the man had been spirited away into hiding. His master was angry and defiant. Mary lost patience and determined to do what she had never done before—bring up the armed forces of the Protectorate to reinforce her own authority.

The slave, meanwhile, escaped to the mission house, but Mary was not mollified. Leaving the villagers quaking in fear of some drastic punitive action, and taking the poor wretch with her, she went to Duke Town to consult Sir Claude Macdonald. He agreed to send up a Vice-Consul with some pomp and ceremony to impress the people with the power of the new administration.

Returning to Ekenge, Mary summoned the local chiefs to meet the official, Ralph Moor. It was a rare excitement when Mr. Moor arrived with a guard of honour who paraded in smart military fashion through the market place. The only drawback to the dignity of the occasion was the fact that the Queen's local representative was found, her skirts tucked up round her, astride the rooftree of her house, tying on fresh palm mats to stop the leaks. "Och, there you are laddie!" she exclaimed, not in the least discomposed.

As a result of this palaver the chiefs promised—as the Creek Town chiefs had done sixteen years earlier—that twins should henceforth be given into the care of the Mission and that there should be no further killing for the dead or for witchcraft. Mary was not so simple as to imagine this would put an immediate end to "murderous practices", but she had brought officials and chiefs together without fear, and this was a step forward.

A treat was in store for her in the new year. Early in 1895 there came up the track from Calabar River someone as unique and unforgettable as Mary herself. Dressed, astonishingly, in the same fur toque, stiff-necked blouse, serge skirt and button boots she was accustomed to wear in England (since she felt it was not decent to go about Africa in clothes one would not dare to wear in Piccadilly) Mary Henrietta Kingsley, niece of the novelist, Charles Kingsley, arrived, intent on making Miss Slessor's acquaintance.

The meeting of these two women seems to have been one of those extraordinary convergences of people and ideas that have a marked significance for their time. They came, as it were, from opposite poles yet found themselves in surprising accord. Together they exemplified all that was best in British attitudes towards Africa.

At thirty-two, Mary Kingsley was the younger by fourteen years. Until two years earlier she had led the life of dutiful domesticity endured by even the most brilliant of Victorian unmarried daughters, and perfectly in keeping with her quaintly sedate appearance. But her appearance utterly deceived. Not only was she unlikely to suffer fits of vapours at sight of crocodiles, scorpions or hordes of naked men; she was a woman of infinite resource in emergency. As she wrote of one encounter in the African forest, "There are no policemen around there; you cannot hail a cab and drive away from things." Though paying lip-service, with habitual self-mockery, to the usual emotions — "my heart went into my mouth and my mind went into my heels" — she seems hardly to have known the sensation of fear.

Nowadays a woman of her stamp would probably be described as a journalist. She travelled, she said, "to understand things", and characterised her formidable African journeys as "skylarking and study". She was a self-taught naturalist. With an observant eye and a fund of anthropological knowledge picked up from her father (who, as a sea-surgeon, amassed notes on societies in every continent but Africa) she went "puddling about" the waterways of Guinea after "fish and fetish", and in so doing arrived at forceful, far-reaching conclusions about the future of Britain in Africa.

In 1895 she was on her second journey down the coast. Her description of the first (in *Travels in West Africa*) gives a good notion of what she was like.

> On my first journey out I did not know the Coast and the Coast did not know me, and we mutually terrified each other. I fully expected to get killed by the local nobility and gentry; they thought I was connected with the World Women's Temperance Association, and collecting shocking details for subsequent magic-lantern lectures on the liquor traffic; so fearful misunderstandings arose, but we gradually educated each other, and I had the best of

the affair; for all I had to teach them was that I was only a beetle and fetish hunter and so forth; while they had to teach me a new world, and a very fascinating course of study I found it.

She had made friends on that first voyage with Sir Claude Macdonald and this time travelled out with his wife and spent four months at the Consulate in Calabar. Much of this time she was afloat in the native canoes she had taught herself to manage, searching for specimens of fresh-water fishes in the creeks and mangrove swamps. The rest she devoted to collecting any kind of African lore that came her way, even if it meant stalking the unlighted streets of Duke Town after dark and falling into its treacherously deep drains in the process.

She was not of a religious temper and, with a few marked exceptions, held missionaries and their works in low esteem. She derided their assumption of moral superiority, and their indifference to traditional beliefs and customs, preferring the frank commercialism of the traders' approach to the people. But to those rare individuals so attuned to African life that they could meet African needs in a practical, respectful fashion, with good humour, she paid ungrudging homage.

I made a point on this visit to Calabar of going up-river to see Miss Slessor at Okyon, and she allowed me to stay with her, giving me invaluable help in the matter of fetish and some of the pleasantest days in my life. This very wonderful lady has been eighteen years in Calabar; for the last six or seven living entirely alone, as far as white folks go, in a clearing in the forest near to one of the principal villages of the Okyon district and ruling as a veritable white chief over the entire Okyon district. Her great abilities, both physical and intellectual, have given her among the savage tribe an unique position, and won her, from white and black who know her, a profound esteem. Her knowledge of the native, his language, his ways of thought, his diseases, his difficulties, and all that is his, is extraordinary, and the amount of good she has done no man can fully estimate.

For one insatiably curious, Miss Kingsley chose a good moment to arrive in Okoyong, for she walked (in her button boots) straight into the middle of a "twin palaver".

When I had the honour of being with Miss Slessor at Okyon, the first twins in that district were saved with their mother from immolation owing entirely to Miss Slessor's great influence with the natives and her own unbounded courage and energy. The mother in this case was a slave woman—an Eboe, the most expensive and valuable of slaves. She was the property of a big woman who had always treated her—as indeed most slaves are treated in Calabar—with great kindness and consideration, but when these two children arrived all was changed; immediately she was subjected to torrents of virulent abuse, her things were torn from her, her china basins, possessions she valued most highly, were smashed, her clothes were torn, and she was driven out as an unclean thing. Had it not been for the fear of incurring Miss Slessor's anger, she would, at this point, have been killed with her children, and the bodies thrown into the bush.

As it was she was hounded out of the village. The rest of her possessions were jammed into an empty gin case and cast to her. No one would touch her, as they might not touch to kill. Miss Slessor had heard of the twins' arrival and had started off, barefooted and bareheaded, at that pace she can go down a bush path. By the time she had gone four miles she met the procession, the woman coming to her and all the rest of the village yelling and howling behind her. On the top of her head was the gin case, into which the children had been stuffed, on the top of them the woman's big brass skillet, and on top of that her two market calabashes. Needless to say, on arriving Miss Slessor took charge of affairs, relieving the unfortunate, weak, staggering woman from her load and carrying it herself, for no one else would touch it, or anything belonging to those awful twin things, and they started back together to Miss Slessor's house in the forest-clearing, saved by that tact which, coupled with her courage, has given Miss Slessor an influence and a power among the negroes unmatched in its way by any other white.

She did not take the twins and their mother down the village path to her own house, for though, had she done so, the people of Okyon would not have prevented her, yet so polluted would the path have been, and so dangerous to pass down, that they would have been compelled to cut another, no light task in that bit of forest, I assure you. So Miss Slessor stood waiting in the broiling sun, in the hot season's height, while a path was being cut to enable her just to get through to her own grounds. The natives worked away hard, knowing it saved the polluting of a long stretch of market road, and when it was finished Miss Slessor went to her own house by it and attended with all kindness, promptness and skill, to the woman and children. I arrived in the middle of this affair, for my first meeting with Miss Slessor, and things at Okyon were rather crowded, one way and another, that afternoon. All the attention one of the children wanted—the boy, for there was a boy and a girl—was burying, for the people who had crammed them into the box had utterly smashed the child's head. The other child was alive, and is still a member of that household of rescued children, all of whom owe their lives to Miss Slessor.

With the care of the woman, a native of Bende to the north, and of the baby girl—this child held in such horror that, whenever it was out of the hands of one or other of the white women, onlookers tumbled over one another in a stampede to escape from the compound—there can have been little formality in the meeting of the two Marys. Although, in the 1890s, there was an inescapable distinction between one brought up "a lady", as Mary Kingsley had been, and a "plain working woman" like Mary Slessor, they were delighted with one another. Mary Kingsley recognised a fellow rebel, who shared her taste for rough adventure and her scorn for those who only touched Africa, as it were, with gloved fingers. Afterwards she spoke of "roustabouts like Mary Slessor and me". They were two of a kind, not only in their readiness for action and danger but for ravelled, time-consuming encounters with African modes of thought.

Mary Kingsley's youthful labours in transcribing her father's notes had prepared her mind for this last hazard as Mary Slessor's education had not. She believed that in Africa, even as "you walk along a narrow line of security with gulfs of murder looming on each side . . . you are as safe as if you were in your easy chair at home, *as long as you get sufficient holding ground*: not on rock, in the bush village inhabited by murderous cannibals, but on ideas in those men's and women's minds; and these ideas which I think I may say you will always find give you safety." She had seen the older woman walk this narrow line in the incident of the twins and was eager to learn from her.

What the presence of such a stimulating and sympathetic visitor meant to the isolated missionary can easily be guessed. She described it with feeling as "the beauty and instruction and joy of those days of companionship". For Miss Kingsley the cheerful tumult of women and children and callers was an amusing change from the ordered peace of the Consul-General's establishment. From affairs of state—Sir Claude was at that moment putting down an uprising at Brass—her attention was drawn to the everyday life of Africa which she portrayed with as good an understanding as any writer of that period. There were constant calls on her hostess's attention, but things were quieter than usual because of the dread presence of the twin-mother and child. Anticipating disaster, the people kept their distance. Even Chief Edem complained, "I cannot go any more to my Mother's house, no never any more."

The two women sat up late at night on the high verandah, deep in discussion, and there was much to make the exchange provocative. Mary Kingsley disapproved of the Mission's all-out attack on African customs which she herself—never squeamish—viewed with delighted appreciation. She also believed that missions exerted too much influence on home opinion and propagated a falsely dark picture of native society. Her passage on the subject of polygamy divertingly describes the moral dilemma of the convert:

One case in the Rivers I know of is almost tragic if you put yourself in his place. An old chief, who had three wives, profoundly and vividly believed that exclusion from the Holy Communion meant an eternal damnation. The missionary had instructed him in the details of this damnation thoroughly, and the chief did not like the prospect at all; but on the other hand he did not like to turn off the three wives he had lived with for years. He found the matter was not even to be compromised, by turning off two and going to church to be married with accompanying hymns and orange blossoms with number three, for the ladies held together; not one of them would marry him and let the other two go, so the poor old chief worried himself to a shammock and anybody else he could get to listen to him. His white trader friends told him not to be such an infernal ass. Some of his black fellow chiefs said the missionary was quite right, and the best thing for him to do would be to hand over to them the three old wives and go and marry a young girl from the mission school. Personally they were not yet afflicted with scruples on the subject of polygamy, and of course (being "missionary man" now) he would not think of taking anything for his wives, so they would do their best, as friends, to help him out of the difficulty. Others of his black fellow chiefs, less advanced in culture, just said: "What sort of fool palaver you make!" and spat profusely. The poor old man smelt hell fire and cried "yo, yo, yo," and beat his hands upon the ground. Still, do not imagine the mission-field is full of yo-yoing old chiefs; for although the African is undecided, he is also very ingenious, particularly in dodging inconvenient moral principles.

Miss Kingsley also took issue with missionaries on the matter of the drink trade, coming down firmly on the side of the traders in saying that imported spirits were of good quality and that drunkenness was not a problem of any dimensions. She insisted that, since "No one who knows me on the Coast will give me a good character for keeping out of bush villages or native quarters of Coast towns", she must have seen it, had it been there.

It is some measure of the two women that their differences on matters they both held deeply important did not prevent the warmest friendship forming. The traveller, born sceptic and lacking in her heart any strong sense of direction, envied the missionary her deep guiding faith. The missionary seems to have decided that the traveller was, whatever her protestations, a Christian under the skin because of the "sincerity of her desire to live for the highest ends and to be some use to others". When asked later to comment on Mary Kingsley's "anti-missionary" position, she put up a spirited defence of her friend, not even shrinking from her views on polygamy.

. . . she would, like Mohammed, allow polygamy until Christianity worked out its own ideals (in Africa) by its own evolution. The only fear she had for Africa's future was the tacking on, as it were, by creeds of any kind, or governments, or false ideas as to the dignity of labour, of a kind of spurious civilisation and a Christianity which should denationalise the race and keep it from assimilating . . . those foreign elements which should form dynamic forces for their evolution as a distinct race . . .

As to the drink traffic:

When she lived with me my people were steeped in drink; it could not be exaggerated as an evil, a gigantic evil, but though I told her so she did not *see* it, and therefore she said, "I can't tell what I have *not* seen. I have seen more drink in evidence in London in one evening than I have seen up to this time on the Coast." I did not take her to the homes and haunts where those things were to be seen because she did not come for temperance statistics, and I had my regular work; moreover, we had a twin baby which frightened everybody and ostracised us in a sense for the time being.

Mary Kingsley made her way back to Calabar and from there on to the Gaboon and an extended journey up the Ogowe River, collecting much valuable material and risking her life in a series of hair-raising episodes which her style of telling transformed into high comedy. She paid a fleeting visit to Ekenge the following October on her return passage to England. This was the last time the two women met.

Their friendship grew in letters, however. Following the publication of *Travels in West Africa*, Mary Kingsley became a public figure, consulted by statesmen, in demand for lectures, lionised at social gatherings. She railed against the smug ignorance of colonial officials and the lack of information about Africa in high places and continued to oppose what she believed to be the one-sided influence of the "missionary party". Yet she kept in touch with the remote household in Okoyong. Her book paid this tribute to Mary, the administrator:

> The instance of what one white can do would give many important lessons in West Coast administration and development. Only the sort of man Miss Slessor represents is rare. There are but few who have the same power of resisting the malarial climate, and of acquiring the language, and an insight into the negro mind, so perhaps after all it is no great wonder that Miss Slessor stands alone, as she certainly does.

In 1900 the correspondence came to an end. The dispassionate Miss Kingsley offered up her life as simply and sacrificially as the early saints of Calabar. When, throwing up the lively intellectual life of London, she went out to the Cape to nurse prisoners taken in the Boer War, she described it as another "odd job" — but she was dead of enteric fever after only two months. It was as if she had flung down of her own accord a life which the storms, fevers, and *jujus* of the Guinea coast had refused to wrest from her.

From the Cross River she had hoped to revisit, Mary Slessor wrote:

> I cannot yet realise that no more letters are to come, and that the long promised visit is never to be paid, and that "something" which we were to attempt together is only to remain a dream.

She contributed a guinea — no mean sum — towards a memorial for the friend who was regarded as an enemy of missionaries. But what that "something" was that these two were to attempt together we shall never know — only that it could not have been ordinary.

10

THE WHITE MA WHO LIVED ALONE

THE NEXT YEAR was a tragic and terrible one for Mary. Little wonder she looked back on the interlude with Mary Kingsley as a "sweet dream".

She suffered a collapse, probably from extreme exhaustion, at the end of 1895. Taken to Duke Town for nursing, she found her old friend William Anderson, now eighty-three, who had come out of retirement to revisit Calabar for the fiftieth anniversary of the Mission, and was with him when he died a few weeks later. The *Record*, always strong on death-bed scenes, printed Mary's description of his passing.

Hugh Goldie, too, had died in the preceding weeks. Both were a personal loss to Mary, the last of the pioneer-mentors of her early days.

There was a sad sequel to the episode of the twins. The surviving baby grew plump and charming and entirely conquered Mary's heart. Mary named her, as she did favourite children, after one of her sisters — Susan. The older girls made a great pet of her, and even Iye, the outcast slave mother, gradually overcame her horror of the twin-child. But at fourteen months old, Susie grabbed at a jug of boiling water, poured it over herself, and was severely scalded.

For two weeks she lingered between life and death while the heart-broken Mary nursed her in her arms day and night. Having, for once, an assistant who could care for the other children — a Miss Murray, from the linen mills, had volunteered for Okoyong but soon failed in health and was gone — Mary walked to Creek Town with the child in her arms in a last desperate attempt to save her. But the doctor could do nothing and she returned to Ekenge the same night. A day or so later, early in the morning, the small sufferer slipped away.

Mary had buried many a pathetic scrap of humanity in the little grave-yard behind the mission house, but this time she could scarcely contain her grief. She laid Susie in her coffin dressed in a white pinafore, put a flower in her hand and her own necklace around the small neck. She could not bear to read the burial service but sat indoors looking out while Miss Murray took her place. The villagers, accustomed to say, "What's a dead child? You can have hundreds of those!" were awestruck at the white mother's suffering. To friends at home Mary wrote, "My heart aches for my darling . . . Oh, the empty place and the silence and the vain longing for the sweet voice and the soft caress and the funny ways. Oh, Susie! Susie!"

She drew close to Iye, the slave mother, and began to save the money to buy her freedom. Mary rarely bought a slave, even for that purpose, since the motive was not generally understood, but she did eventually free Iye, at a cost of ten pounds. The woman could not have been sold to anyone else, Mary explained, except perhaps to cannibal tribes for "chop", because a twin-mother had "no character". Everyone held her in fear. For the same reason Mary could not train her for school or dispensary work. She hoped to make her a good house-servant and, in fact, found her useful as an interpreter when the time came to move north-west towards the country from which Iye came.

But if the year was marked by private distress, the public scene gave some reason for satisfaction. Looking back over her time at Okoyong and using the "we" that signified she was never alone in her efforts, she wrote, in her report to the Mission Board:

> . . . for fully a year we have heard of nothing like violence from even the most backward of our people. They have thanked me for restraining them in the past, and begged me to be their consul, as they neither wished black man nor white man to be their king. It would be impossible, apart from a belief in God's particular and personal providence in answer to prayer, to account for the ready obedience and submission to our judgment which was accorded to us. It seemed sometimes to be almost miraculous that hordes of armed, drunken, passion-swayed men would give heed and chivalrous homage to a woman, and one who had neither wealth nor outward display of any kind to produce the slightest sentiment in her favour. But such was the case and we do not recollect one instance of insubordination.

Her ambition to "make human life safe" had been in some measure achieved. "There seems", she wrote, "to have dawned on them the fact that life is worth saving, even at the risk of one's own." Drink also was on the decrease.

The women still drink, but it is at home where the husband can keep them in check. In our immediate neighbourhood it is an extremely rare thing to see a woman intoxicated, even on feast days and at funerals . . . We have also noted a decided stand being taken by several of the young mothers who have been our friends and scholars against it being given by husbands or visitors to their children.

In the field of education:

School teaching has been carried on under great difficulty owing to the scattered population, the family quarrels which made it formerly a risk to walk alone, the fear of sorcery and of the evil spirits which are supposed to dwell in the forest, the denseness of the forest itself, which makes it dangerous for children to go from one place to another without an armed escort, the withdrawing of the girls when they have just been able to read in order to go to their seclusion and fattening, and the consequent drafting of them to great distances to their husband's farms, the irregular attendance of boys who accompany their masters wherever they go, and who take the place of postmen and news-agents-general to the country.

She then went on to describe the "multifarious claims" on a single-handed missionary, from keeping house utterly without those services taken for granted in Europe, to nursing the sick, succouring fugitives and sorting out quarrels while ". . . all the bothersome and, to European notions, stupid details of native etiquette are to be observed if we are to win the favour and confidence of the people. Moreover . . . we must make and keep in repair buildings, fences, drainage, etc. and all amid surroundings in which the climate and its forces are leagued against us." Mud buildings roofed with raffia palm were quickly destroyed by storms from without and white ants from within, and needed constant attention.

Anyone visiting Okoyong could see that the beginning of a peaceful and productive life had been made and that it was the lone white woman's ascendancy over the people that kept the bad old customs in check. Time now, one might have thought, for her to consolidate the gains — erect permanent buildings and improve the ramshackle mission house where, in marked contrast to the ways of most of the Scottish mission stations, meals happened at any old hour and the roof might be repaired, or the walls be mudded, at midnight or at dawn.

But, though she was now nearly fifty, it was no part of Mary's

ambition to achieve a more ordered life for herself and her family, or
to live in matriarchal calm amidst the once unruly, now manageable,
"heirs of salvation". Contemplation of what God, through her, had
wrought suggested to her mind only the greater work that awaited
her. In short, she felt it was time to move.

Her people, in search of better land for their crops, had shifted
gradually westwards, so that Ekenge was no longer at the heart of
Okoyong. Mary obtained permission to transfer her station to
Akpap, where there was a busy market place. The new site would
be six miles from Ikunetu, a trading village on the Cross River, the
nearest point from which help, mail and supplies could be got up
to the mission. After some initial reluctance on this account, the
Committee approved the move and resolved to build her a house
of permanent materials and a storage shed beside the river.

Mary could not wait for these splendours, however. She found a
two-room mud hut at Akpap, with a rough lean-to shelter for cooking and washing in and, with her numerous family, took up residence
under conditions little better than those of her first year at Ekenge.

Only now she was virtual ruler of Okoyong, so that her wretched
hut was, to all intents and purposes, its seat of government. From
it she and her girls held classes, dispensed medicines and arbitrated
disputes. Sessions of the native court were held there. It served, like
all her other houses, as an orphanage. Half a dozen babies to care
for, all of them precious to "Ma", were quite usual. But the odds
against them were fearsome.

This is the last night of the year, though one has to be reminded
of the fact, as there is no outward sign of it in our bush home . . .
I had a dear motherless baby boy at the time your box came. One
day I had rather severe fever and could not see to him; everybody was laid up with colds in the head and fever, something like
your influenza, and I begged the girls not to take the children
outside — they however, to spare me the noise, took them out, and
dear wee Bobby got a cold which turned to phthisis, and in
October he went "up higher". We laid his body in the garden at
the new house, the first grave we have there; and the first thing
next morning there was a motherless girlie to be taken in his place.
Her mother ate poison bean the previous day in Calabar, and
died. Then came two wee twin girlies who were strong enough
likely to live. Fever again, and they, too, after a fortnight of struggle,
went to Jesus. I felt so utterly depressed, I had to keep working
hard to keep my spirits up at all. Then came a visit from a Euro-

pean who had a Government post, and has great opportunities and as great interest in the governing of the natives, and I took the full benefit of his presence to get some reforms and laws carried out. There was a deal of writing about this; and then came another couple of babies. Another fever, and one of them went again; and by God's good hand on us we have been struggling to keep things going and to save the other darling, who is thriving nicely now. So you see the loss of infant life through want of help! It is so saddening . . . I keep very good health; it is only after the walk for the twins, or some extra spell of fatigue, that I get fever, I am thankful to say that I have easily recovered from every attack during this dry season. It is the want of sleep, I daresay, which makes me susceptible, for I get very little sleep with the babies to nurse; but with it I am as well as I would be in Britain, so if no help comes I shall go on till I feel I *must* give up . . .

The loss of these four babies was succeeded by a calamitous smallpox epidemic which swept through the district in the spring. Mary vaccinated all she could. Then, when her supply of lymph was exhausted, she inoculated others from the scabs of those whose inoculation had "taken". Mr. Alexander, engineer of the launch *David Williamson*, who called in regularly with mails and supplies, found her doing it with a penknife!

Of the villages around, Ekenge was the worst stricken. Mary went back and opened up her old house to use as a hospital. The sick packed into it, but all who were uninfected fled the village so that there was no one to help with the nursing or to bury the dead. Not a soul would lend a hand—not wives or husbands, slaves or children, of the dying.

The victims were old acquaintances—Chief Ekpenyong whom she had worried into giving up the poison beans, all those years ago, then his brother, Chief Edem. Mary had owed much to Edem's protection and friendship over the years but her struggle to save him was in vain. When he died in the middle of the night, she herself knocked together a coffin for the chief who had been so peculiarly her own, dug his grave, and laid him to rest. Not for him the plumes and silks and mirrors and sacrificial cow that had gone into the grave of his dead son and seemed to him so barbarously insufficient. No magic-lantern show marked his passing.

She left a dead village and a house full of corpses when, an hour or two before dawn, she dragged herself back through the darkness to Akpap, totally exhausted.

The epidemic had burnt itself out locally but from further inland came tragic tales of its ravages, for as people fled from one place, leaving the dying behind, they carried the infection to the next. Mary demanded the Calabar Committee's approval for her to go up and help, for it seemed to her that God had taken her four babies expressly to leave her free for this terrible task.

But the Mission Committee was determined she should take her furlough. They knew from Charles Ovens, who had gone up to start work on the new house, that her strength was spent. Mr. Ovens's cheery presence helped make life supportable but, as half of the tiny house was given over to him, Mary and the children were more cramped for space than ever. It was certainly unhealthy as well as uncomfortable, for Mr. Ovens told how, in the gloom of his windowless room, he reached for what he took to be a sponge floating in the wash-basin and found it was a dead rat!

Mary balked at going on leave without someone to take her place but was at last persuaded that her life was at stake. As the excellent Charles Ovens could keep an eye on things, it was as good a time as any, though the children couldn't be left with him as with a lady agent. After five years so cut off from the world, the thought of home brought little joy to Mary. She shrank from a return to the "conventionalities and all the paraphernalia of civilisation".

Friends in Duke Town were appalled to find that, sick as she was, she intended taking four girls home to Scotland with her. Iye, two babies, and several girls were deposited on another missionary, but she felt she could not leave Maggie, Alice and Mary, all under five, or Janie, now sixteen. Not one of the four, nor Mary herself, owned any garment but the one they stood up in. Mary felt sure God would provide. And, sure enough, a box from Glasgow arrived with enough woollen material in it for capable friends to run up wardrobes for the entire party.

Mary was too exhausted to plan for the weeks ahead. Her friends, the M'Crindles, at Joppa, received no warning of the invasion about to take place until they received a telegram from Liverpool asking them to meet Mary at Waverley Station. They must have swallowed hard when four black youngsters tumbled out of the railway carriage, all but stopping traffic on the station platform! The children spoke little English and had no conception of European life, which must have been remarkably uncomfortable for all concerned. But as soon as she had strength to match her will, Mary found a small house at Seton Mill, where they could live after their own fashion.

Here, by the sea, Mary and the children ran barefoot and ate and slept as suited them. The five-year-old, named after Mary, even picked up enough English to attend school in Portobello. But their ménage undoubtedly appeared squalid to Mary's friends, who would find her, subject as she was to recurrent bouts of fever, shivering by the fire, clearly in need of rest and care and a sound diet.

Miss Nora Adam was secretary of the Zenana Committee which now had charge of all the Mission's work among women. A woman of private means, she gave largely of her own income to provide rest homes for missionaries and also treats of a personal kind, like the occasional stay in a comfortable hotel. She and Mary were warm friends and it was doubtless to her that Mary owed her ability to support such numbers of children and raise the not inconsiderable cost of their passages to England.

On this occasion, Miss Adam swept the whole household off to Bowden St. Boswells, where she lived and maintained several houses for the use of missionaries on leave. Here Mary recuperated. Before long she was again taking her place on the speaker's platform in churches up and down Scotland.

If photographs are to be believed, Mary had never been more attractive, nor personally more compelling, than she was now. The candour of her youthful portraits had matured into an expression warm and wise. The boyish face was pared to the bone and, under the sallow transparency of skin that is the mark of tropical life, the delicate bone structure was revealed. One looks in vain, remembering how she drove her failing body over rough bush tracks, or, single-handed and exhausted, buried the smallpox dead, for signs of fanaticism or self-punishing pride. But the face is that of a loving mother, full of amused understanding. Her slight stature and gentle manner were remarked on and the sweetness of her voice.

She had only to stand up on a platform and speak of her experiences to have money come raining in. Yet, inexplicably, she still could not bring herself to address a male audience—she who could be terse with government officials, sarcastic with her missionary brethren and imperious with chiefs. A single male arrival once caused her to stop speaking and murmur, "If the gentleman in the meeting would hide behind the lady in front of him I would be more at ease." Another time she rushed off the platform and could not be coaxed back.

And the one thing she wanted most from the home Church was not forthcoming. She complained that the Calabar Mission called for money, and *got* money — "of great value in its place" — but not men and women. Specifically she wanted an ordained minister for Okoyong. "I feel that my work there is done. I can teach them no more. I would like to go further inland and make a home among a tribe of cannibals."

She had every reason to expect, when this season of travelling was over, that her particular pleading for Okoyong would bear fruit. She had made a deep impression everywhere. The Board would have liked her to extend her speaking tour but she was desperately anxious to get back to her unmanned station. "If ye dinna send me back, I'll swim back!" An interview with a Reuters correspondent, as she embarked on the *Oron* in December 1898, brought her story before a much wider public than ever before. To the ship's company she was already a celebrity. They did everything they could to make Christmas aboard happy for her and the children.

According to the *Record*, an unnamed Scotswoman travelled with them, "to help in the care and training of rescued children". It is not clear whether she was unnamed because too humble to rate formal appointment or, as seems more likely, because Mary had hired her entirely on her own initiative. Possibly she had decided, with the help of private donations, to start the kind of child-care centre she had advocated for eighteen years at Akpap.

The immense interest that had been shown in her work made the isolation of the next months especially hard to bear. The good permanent house stood ready and fit for the most fastidious mission couple, but the expected arrivals never came. For three years, dogged by ill health, she struggled on and never once left her station even to visit Calabar. The anonymous Scotswoman cannot have lasted long, for she was never mentioned again.

The chronic failure of the Mission, even shorthanded as it was, to send reinforcements to hold the ground Mary had occupied is hard to fathom. In 1895, after seven whole years of spadework, she was obliged to write: ". . . as no ordained minister has ever been resident or available for more than a short visit, no observance of the ordinances of Baptism or the Lord's Supper have been held and we have not had the usual definite offers of persons as candidates for Church membership." Mary walked to Creek Town and back by night to get medical help or tinned milk for her babies, yet it was apparently impossible to provide regular pastoral visits from there or from Adiabo, even nearer. And so it remained for many years.

It is easier to understand the lack — except for very brief periods — of the companion-in-harness that was usual in the field of women's work. Later colleagues declared that, though they loved Miss Slessor, they couldn't work with her. Her methods were too personal and her way of life too haphazard to permit of help. She had no set routine and was thought wantonly careless in her disregard of such vital health precautions as boiling the drinking water. By this time the mosquito was known to be the carrier of malaria, but Mary would use no net. The children who came to her in all stages of illness were not isolated as in other mission establishments, so all suffered alike from malaria and such prevalent debilitating diseases as dysentery.

Nor were Mary's hard-working girls particular in points of hygiene. Visitors (and there was an appeal in the easy-going style of life that kept visitors coming, regardless of peril to health) knew not to expect meals at any given time. When hungry, they would call Janie and ask for "chop". And Janie was known to take the chicken from the cooking pot and lay it on the mud floor while she made gravy.

Mary was inured to the flies, mosquitoes, cockroaches and rats that other mission ladies set themselves strenuously to combat. In later years her devoted friend, Miss Peacock, shared a mud dais with Mary and was unable to sleep for the rats. Mary swore it was her imagination. "There're nae rats here!" But next night, bumped by her restless visitor, she flung out an arm in her sleep, as of habit, crying, "Git out, ye brute!" and when Miss Peacock came to breakfast with a black eye, was very penitent indeed.

Mary's indifference in matters of bed and board were, of course, the secret of her mobility. No limitations of time or finance or prior responsibility could be allowed to stand in the way of her essential mission. But this unfitted her for teamwork, so that she was fated to go it alone.

As help failed to materialise, her frustration mounted. She longed to press inland, leaving the consolidation of her work to others, but until she was relieved this was out of the question. She was highly-strung, in spite of her saving sense of the ridiculous, and began to sleep badly. Her temper suffered and some of the gaiety went out of her. In court, her patience quickly gave out, particularly if she felt witnesses were attempting to deceive her. An administrative officer once saw her flailing a chief of some importance over the head with his own umbrella for telling lies in answer to his question. But the victim of her wrath seldom commanded any public sympathy since she was felt to be just.

She was ill almost from the time of her return and for three months could not leave her bed. As early as June 1899 the Mission Secretary in Edinburgh felt compelled to write *insisting* that she permit a mission doctor to visit her and report on her health. There must have been a very real likelihood of her being invalided home, possibly for good. For Mary this was a truly fearful prospect. Britain meant little to her now. All her ties were in Africa. In the increasingly frequent sleepless nights she agonised over her children.

"How could I leave the bairns in this dreadful land?" she wrote. "Who would mother them in this sink of iniquity?" And then again: "I do not think I could bear the parting with my children again. If I be spared a few years more I shall have a bit of land and build a wee house of my own near one of the principal stations, and just stay out my days there with my bairns and lie down among them."

It is unlikely that Mission or government would have sanctioned such a plan. Nor would the Africans have given her any rest in her retirement. She was social dynamite in any African community. Yet, though she was that phenomenon in Africa, a single independent woman, "the white ma who lived alone", she was nevertheless a mother who could not forsake her children nor make plans only for herself. And so the problem haunted her. The only solution was to gather up her failing strength in defiance of weakness and press on, and this was what she did.

II

BAIRNS IN BOXES

THE BABIES BROUGHT to Mary in calabashes and milk boxes, or picked up by her from the wayside, were beginning to grow up, while others still came and one or two stayed. She was staggeringly maternal. Her love for children was boundless and undiminishing. To the end of her life she was seldom without a child in her arms.

A milestone was reached in December 1899 when seventeen-year-old Janie, now usually called Jean, married Akiba Eyo, the Mission's star pupil. Mary performed the ceremony. The bridegroom appears to have been a slave of Ma Eme's household, for the civil form of the contract entered in the marriage register concluded: "They went to the farm with Eme Ete."

Though Mary described Jean's husband as "not of the highest social standing" she was content with the match. The young man had been trained by her and was highly popular with the whole household. But to Jean, reared alternately in cramped hovels and airy mission houses, on ocean liners and in the plain but ordered comfort of Scottish Christian homes — to settle down in an African compound must have been a strange experience.

Yet it is surprising she found a man brave enough to marry her. A Nigerian Pastor, Nwachuku Eme, has described how, even as late as 1943, his family received the news that he intended marriage with a twin:

> The mere thought of bringing a twin girl into the compound was itself an evil; how much more bringing her as a wife to live in the compound. He (my father) then started to narrate the misfortune and curses that would come upon any man who attempted what I was trying to do. Such a person, according to him, would be childless, would not have any success in life, and finally would die a miserable death . . .

Jean's marriage was intended to be a living witness to the truth of Mary's teaching that all men and women are as one in the sight of God. They should be an example of Christian partnership, too, for

Jean was not the White Ma's daughter for nothing, and was well able to stand up for herself.

It began happily. Akiba Eyo, true to his training, made no objection to Jean spending much of her time at the Mission to help with the babies, nor to her bringing back an occasional one to their home to tend while she did her housework. He did not demur at her handling twins. But when Jean herself gave birth to a baby which died, the marriage foundered. Evidently the young husband took fright at the apparent working-out of the twin taboo and would have no more to do with her. The bride returned to the mission house and took up her old tasks while her breasts were still heavy with milk.

Jean had long been Mary's right hand, almost an extension of herself, and Mary had been hard put to manage without her during the brief months of her marriage. "I have only three girls at present and I have nine babies, and what with the washing and the school and the palavers and the visitors, you may be sure there are no drones in this house."

Jean was the most intelligent and capable of the girls, disciplined, good-tempered and with sufficient authority to keep the younger members in line. Adopted before Mary's own responsibilities became overwhelming, she had had more personal, uninterrupted schooling than the rest, and two periods in Britain when she had Mary all to herself. Congregations in Scotland took a particular, personal interest in her upbringing and one letter from the Mission Secretary suggests that there may even have been a move to educate her there (which he, however, was quick to discourage). Her English was good. She was a voracious reader, particularly of Scottish newspapers, and she and Mary had playful tussles over any fresh book or magazine that arrived in the post, to the wondering admiration of the unlettered younger children.

Everyone who knew Mary knew Jean. She was self-effacing and loyal, half daughter, half handmaiden. Mary drove her hard. She was only going on eight when she accompanied Mary to Devonshire in 1891 and looked after her through a long convalescence. Back in Okoyong she carried stern messages to angry chiefs, trotted off to bring back babies who were reported abandoned, and stood in for Mary in every conceivable emergency. In time she became bold enough to shield Mary from importunate callers, scolding them with, "Is she never to have time to eat?" and "You are killing Ma with your foolish ways!"

She taught school, nursed the sick and ran the house. It was to

Jean that Mary issued provisions and gave out market money—the thin brass rods or clumsy, horseshoe-shaped *manillas* that were the local currency. Yet only Dr. Hitchcock, when Mary was old and ill, commented on the quality of the woman: "Wonderful Jean!" he called her.

Jean became an able evangelist, who might have emerged as a leader of the people in her own right. But she outlived Mary by only three years, dying in the great flu epidemic of 1918.

Nearly all the children close to Mary were given European names, possibly to satisfy a personal nostalgia, possibly out of a sense that African names were of their nature "heathen" and would tend to bind them to the old ways. It was common at this time, anyway, for Africans to adopt European names as they became educated or were baptised—a process sharply reversed half a century later.

Annie, slow-witted and placid, but strong, was, at the time of Jean's marriage, entering her teens. She had shown no aptitude for learning but loved growing things. To her fell the heavy outdoor chores. She cleared and dug every spare inch of mission land in order to grow yams and cassava, beans, corn, peppers and greens for the family table. Annie later married a Christian trader, produced the first live "grandchild" and gave, with her husband, loyal support to Mary in her last years.

Next in age came Mary's namesake, born the 2nd February, 1893. Mary left an account of her—a sort of birth certificate—which showed the intricate working of custom in matters of marriage and child-custody. As a new-born baby she was the pawn in a long-drawn out dispute between the clan of her dead mother and that of her father. The father at last disclaimed all responsibility for her and abandoned her by the roadside.

The story of her rescue was told by Mary Kingsley:

Her mother died a few days after her birth, so the child was taken and thrown into the bush by the side of the road that led to the market. This was done one market-day some distance from Okyon town. This particular market is held every ninth day, and on the succeeding market-day some women from the village by the side of Miss Slessor's house happened to pass along the path and heard the child feebly crying: they came into Miss Slessor's yard in the evening, and sat chatting over the day's shopping, etc., and casually mentioned in the way of conversation that they heard the child crying, and that it was rather remarkable it should still be alive. In a marvellous way it had been left by the leopards and snakes, with which this bit of forest abounds, and, more marvellous still, the driver ants had not scented it. Other ants had considerably eaten into it one way and another; nose, eyes, etc., were swarming with them and with flies; the cartilage of the nose and part of the upper lip had been absolutely eaten into, but in spite of this she is now one of the prettiest black children I have ever seen, which is saying a good deal, for negro children are very pretty ...

The chief of the clan to which the mother had belonged snorted derisively, "Make her live!" when Mary offered the child back to him. "But," Miss Kingsley commented, "When Miss Slessor had had all the trouble of it the natives had no objection to pet and play with it, calling it 'the child of wonder' because of its survival."

The child of wonder, (third to bear the name Mary Mitchell Slessor) grew up light-hearted and gay. She acquired some education, even attending school briefly in Scotland, but was inclined to be dreamy. She was a fetching young thing, however, who attracted numbers of suitors and seems to have been a special favourite with her white mother.

There were two younger girls—stolid, stammering, Bible-reading Alice, and the unstable "flibberty-gibbet", Maggie. Up to 1900 the permanent "family" had consisted of all girls. Quite evidently it was girl children who were most in need of rescue. Soon after Jean's return home, however, a new-born orphan boy was confided to Mary's care by a leading chief of the district, Okon Ekpo.

Jean nursed the child at her still-full breast and named him after the son of the manse in Bowden St. Boswells, whom she had had the honour of carrying to church for his christening. And so he became Daniel MacArthur Slessor, a name he bears proudly to this day, and even in the nationalist fervour of the fifties refused to exchange for any other.

His recollections begin with the house at Akpap. As the only boy, he was made much of, so that the people began to call him "Akpan Ma" (Ma's eldest son). Until of school age he was always by her side. When small, he travelled with her on her rounds on the shoulders of an Okoyong carrier. She might be hatless, but *his* head was shielded from the sun with a large tam o' shanter. He tells of her intense concern for him:

At the Mission bungalow at Akpap, while Ma knitted on the wide verandah I lay almost by her feet, gazing into the distance, waiting to go instantly on errands and generally to minister to her needs. I was then very young but I believe I filled her heart with happiness. There was nothing too difficult to do, there was nothing too hard to discharge. I knew that she got over-anxious when she sent me on errands and her heart beat fast if there was the slightest delay. She would stop all work, glue her eyes down the road, wondering what had happened to the boy. Perhaps I am at times delayed by the Obong, glad to see me, when all the children would rush into the compound to see the miracle which Ma had performed in an orphan. Then on such occasions I would invariably meet her halfway down to town. Oh Dan, she would say in relief, I was wondering what might have befallen you. Then I would explain the cause of the delay. Cheerful and happy again we would return to the bungalow hand in hand, chattering and twittering. As we pass the villagers would all stand and say mournfully, "Mbom oh, Enye eke bine eyen esie" (meaning "Oh, Ma, so she was after her son!")

She dosed the children regularly with quinine, nursed them tenderly in sickness, but was strict in the Scottish fashion and beat them for disobedience. She suffered like any mother for their sorrows and misdoings and preferred, for their safety and her own peace of mind, to cart them about with her under the most trying conditions. In Dan's words:

. . . we lived so happily, a happier family I cannot admit existed. Each time I go to Akpap, I wind my way to the old Mission bungalow, enter from the rear where we were oft to be, climb the creaking steps and review the old rooms in which we used to sleep, the well from which we drank and the little slope where we used to roll and tumble.

At the same time, Mary expected much of her cherished children. They were often her arms and legs, her messengers and porters. They would find themselves deputed to teach a class or rebuke a wrongdoer in her stead. Frequently they had to fend for themselves. But neither in working-class Dundee nor in Africa could children expect to monopolise the attention of their parents or be waited on by them. In both places children took responsible care of their younger siblings. Dan tells of her own passion for work:

No matter how slack times appeared to be, but Ma would think of something to do—from house building to house thatching, putting a wee bit of putty to a leak in the roof; mending a shaky window, getting mud for a broken wall, hoeing and raking the yard, even to going round and pruning trees and shrubs. No, she was never idle, she would become ill if she remained idle, she would say.

No one, he declares, could make better mud walls nor tie wattle stronger than she could. And when it came to roofing with metal sheets, "She would go under the roof and point out where to nail and I would be on top with hammer and nails and nail the zinc home. All the time she would keep saying 'That's the ticket, my boy' as each nail went home . . . Ma could not tolerate a slow worker, she would prefer you stood off than waste her time in a slow progress."

She would not allow her children to tell any untruth, nor to be, as most of the people were, dominated by fear. Dan remembers her saying, after she had refused to be escorted along a bush road at night, "Never allow weakness to overpower you. I know these roads are dangerous but if I were to admit weakness I might as well pack and return to Scotland." Often on their treks she would suddenly push the children behind her and lash out with a stone or bamboo stick to frighten off a leopard or kill a snake. Once a snake coiled up and bit her and she sucked her finger in silence. But Dan's most famous story is of her assault on a hippopotamus:

We were once on the Enyong Creek when she was suddenly disturbed from her reading by shouts of "Ma se isantim" (meaning, Ma, there is a hippo). With the other children I was lying on the bottom of the canoe. Her first concern, as usual, was not to create a fright and excitement among us, lest one might tumble overboard. Calmly she rose to her full height, oblivious of the tossing of the frail craft, tossed her papers aside and, taking a long bamboo stick, she threw it with all her might and shouted out, "Go away, you!" To the utter surprise of the paddlers the hippo dipped, foamed and made away.

The people marvelled that a human being could give orders to a wild beast. But her assaults on the dreaded, weirdly-masked Egbo runners, whom it was considered death for a woman even to *see*, must have seemed to them more daring still. "On several occasions she attacked the dreaded Egbo for frightening her children and tore the mask off the face of one of them. The others showed nice round heels as they sprang into the bush," relates Dan.

Yet the family life was tender and warm. Prayers were said,

twice a day, wherever they were, and hymns sung—to the harmonium while it lasted, and then to the beat of a small skin-covered drum or basketwork rattle—Mary tapping the sleepy children on the head with it if they threatened to doze. A visitor recalled her annoyance when the children admitted they couldn't remember where she had left off in the Bible lesson—and then her laughing contrition when she had to confess, "Isn't it awfu'. I dinna remember myself!" In later days the children themselves conducted these services, in English or Efik, according to their talents.

There were peaceful times when only the arrival of a visitor, or the coming of market day, provided diversion. Pleasures were homemade. Mary would plan a tea party, or a picnic rendezvous with friends from Duke Town.

There were times, in the dripping gloom of the rainy season, when they all got on one another's nerves and there was much quarrelling and bickering. There were gruesome adventures like the time when a murderer, who had escaped trial by torture and was awaiting police escort to Calabar, hanged himself in a ground floor store room of the mission house.

The greatest joy was when a messenger arrived to say that the mission launch had unloaded a box from Scotland at the landing. No knowing what such a box might contain. (We find Mary thanking friends for articles as useless in that climate as tea cosies and woollen scarves!) But there were certain to be things never seen before in Okoyong, and others infinitely precious—needles and buttons, safety pins and cloth and soap, picture books and pens. The whole household would troop to the beach and open the box. Mary would dig deep, excitedly hunting for the tins of toffee and chocolate always included for her and the children.

When they had gazed at everything, the contents of the box would be parcelled into individual head-loads for the children to carry home, where they would be sorted out and distributed at Mary's discretion. There was always something for each child, often addressed to him or her by name by Sunday school children in Scotland who knew them from Mary's vivid letters. But first they would kneel together—white mother and bairns, the freed slave Iye, and all who had trailed down after them—and thank God for his kindness.

When people said Mary "lived native" they referred not only to her preference for mud houses and African food, but to the intimacy of her relations with the children. She did not make the distinction most missionaries did between their private life and service to the

people. Nurslings she took into her own room and bed. When there
were many she had them slung in little hammocks from the rafters,
the strings tied in such a way that she could rock them from where
she lay and herself get some rest.

A friend, happening in on her unexpectedly, found her standing
over four buckets of water warming on the stove. In the buckets
were four babies. Mary washed them absent-mindedly as she talked
and nearly wore them out with scrubbing, in the joy of conversation
with a fellow Scot and Christian. But her first concern was to get
them dried, kissed and put to bed, each in its own padded milk
crate.

Probably no missionary society today would approve of its
workers identifying themselves so closely with their charges, (on the
grounds that it would alienate them from their own society and unfit
them for adult life). In her own time some considered it wiser to
leave the children in their own villages at some risk, urging the
parents to take care of them, than to whisk them into safe-keeping
as Mary did. A great many, it would be pointed out, died anyway.
She was asked why, given her magisterial authority, she did not
order families to accept twins, under pain of prosecution. But like
St. Paul ("... if righteousness come by the law, then Christ is dead
in vain") Mary preferred to use legal pressures sparingly. "After
all," she said, "we are foreigners and they own the country so I
always try to make the law fit in, while we adjust things between us."

Not all of the children she rescued were grateful. Madge White
Slessor, "Whitie", the last twin saved, did not credit that she would
have been killed by her own people and felt her rescue by Miss
Slessor marked her for special derision: "I go to the market and they
know I am a twin, raise two fingers to my face and run away laughing." Mary died before she was very old and without her backing
Whitie was unmarriageable. Though trained as a nurse, she seems,
like many in her case, to have drifted on to the streets.

Alice and Maggie were given mission schooling but may also
have found themselves misfits, having neither Miss Slessor's
capacity for triumphant spinsterhood nor the adaptability to marry
and settle down in an ordinary African household. Asuquo, youngest
of all, ran away from school to sail with the troops in 1914 and was
thereafter something of a rolling stone. When last heard of, he had
come to rest as a cocoa farmer in the Cameroons. Modern psycho-
logy suggests, however, that children as abused and neglected as
these had been at birth would, in any case, have found life an
unequal struggle.

To Dan, the best educated of the family, to have been "Akpan Ma", Mary Slessor's eldest son, has been the great adventure of his life, bringing him contacts all over the world. Marked out by Mary for the Church, he decided on leaving college to join the government service. After a long and creditable career in posts as far apart as Ibadan and Kaduna he returned with his wife and nine children to Calabar where, active as a churchman and journalist, he remains a prominent citizen.

12

THE BREAKING OF THE LONG JUJU

ACROSS THE RIVER to the north-west, between the Cross River and the Niger, lay a large, populous and virtually unknown country. This was the home of the Ibos, known for centuries to slave traders as the source of some of the sturdiest, most intelligent of their cargoes but—since traders, officials and missionaries alike groped inland by way of the river arteries—in 1900 still a blank on the map. Between Iboland and the sea lived the Ibibios, speaking a variant of the Efik language.

Access to this region had long been denied by the power of the Delta chiefs. Even those up-river stations where Europeans had established themselves tended to be outposts of the coastal tribes rather than an integral part of the adjacent country. The only Africans to move freely in and about these districts seem to have been the slave-dealers, many of them agents of the great Ibo god Chuku and members of the Aro tribe.

The Aros were a clever people, numbering some fifty thousand and holding unquestioned sway over a wide region through the power of the mysterious oracle known in pidgin English as "The Long Juju". For centuries they had shipped slaves south through the great market at Itu down the Cross River to the sea, northward across the hills of Bende to the Niger and thence—impossible as it seems—into the slave caravans of the Sahara. The Ibo language could be heard spoken on the Mediterranean coast of Africa, in Virginia, Brazil and Cuba. Professor Dike believes that the bulk of slaves exported from the Cross River were obtained through the agency of the Oracle, more than were obtained by kidnapping and raids. The town (or group of villages) known as Arochuku, where the Oracle was situated, was a few miles from the head of the Enyong Creek, on the doorstep into Ibo country. At the sacred grove, primed by agents who infiltrated nearly every town and village, pilgrims, petitioners and litigants arrived to beg Chuku's favour, or his help in settling quarrels. All practical authority over some hundreds of square miles lay in the hands of the Aro priests.

Their widely scattered agents could give the pilgrims protection on their way and judge to a nicety the extent of their resources, so that the priests at the Oracle would know to the last brass rod, cow or slave, how much they could demand in fee. They also provided an intelligence network which, reinforced by the dread in which the Oracle was held, gave its priests dominion far beyond their own tribal boundaries. They were not themselves a fighting people but, when Chuku demanded sacrifices, there was no lack of subject chiefs bound to raid their weaker neighbours to provide victims. In Ibibio country the fear of capture had become such that organised tribal life had almost ceased, the people having fled in small family groups into the bush.

The Oracle lay in a deep, densely wooded ravine, threaded by a stream and approached down tortuous paths which made it seem much larger than it was. In the eerie light the timid supplicant, when his blindfolds were removed, could make out little but the sacred fish (prominent in every account), with their long suckers and glaring yellow eyes. Beyond two altars, caked with sacrificial blood and topped with skulls, hung screens of palm matting which hid the dark mouth of a cave also encrusted with skulls, and muffled the fearful voice which at intervals issued from it.

"If the charge were one of witchcraft or poisoning and the accused had been found guilty," writes one authority,* "he might be ordered to hand over one of his children to the family of his victim, or to pay heavy damages, or to go home and hang himself." But for centuries the Aros made grimly cynical use of their power. Those whom the Oracle condemned were seized by the priests, manacled and, like thousands before them, marched off by secret paths to be sold into slavery. The stream, dyed with camwood or goat's blood, ran red out of the grotto and the people waiting above believed a fresh victim to have been devoured by an angry god.

In 1900, although the overseas traffic in slaves was long dead and suppressed, there was still little effective control over the trans-*African* slave routes or internal slave trading. The Aros had always driven off those emissaries who, from time to time, tried to make contact, ready to oppose to the death any agreement that might end their lucrative, age-old traffic.

In 1894, Roger Casement, at that time a young vice-consul, tried to explore Aro country and open up trade, but was unable to pene-

* C. K. Meek, *Law and Authority in a Nigerian Tribe*, Oxford University Press, 1937.

trate more than fifteen miles west of the Cross River before being driven off, and was considered lucky to escape with his life.

No action was taken by the government. Neither Sir Claude Macdonald nor his successor, Sir Ralph Moor, believed in the use of force except to bring about a settlement between warring tribes or an end to ritual killings. But as the encroaching power of the Protectorate narrowed down the field of Aro operations, slave raids became more daring and flagrant. In 1900 Sir Ralph prepared to mount an expedition against the Aros in order to put a finish to the inland slave trade and destroy the power of the Long Juju.

Things came to a head after 136 pathetic survivors of a company of 800, who had set out from near the Niger to consult the Long Juju, straggled more dead than alive into the government headquarters in Eket. Their story was told in the Governor's report for 1899:

> They were led about the country by a circuitous route for about three months before reaching the seat of the Long Juju, in a village close to which they were finally made to sit down. Batches of them, about ten to twenty, were occasionally taken away from this village, ostensibly to consult Long Juju; but from events which have since come to light, there can be no doubt that they were victims used for human sacrifices by the Aros themselves, or sold to outlying tribes for that purpose, or as slaves. In this way the party of 800 gradually dwindled down to the miserable residue of 136, who were the most wretched and emaciated body of people I ever saw grouped together. They were evidently regarded as unfit to be disposed of as slaves, or even for purposes of sacrifice; and it must be due, I think, to some extent, to their miserable condition that they had the opportunity of escaping.

It took more than a year to get the expedition—the most spectacular and conclusive of many small military operations carried out in the first years of the century—under way. The Cross River would never be the same. As the Aros leapt to local prominence even old missionary hands like James Luke, who had enthusiastically explored the river region, had to confess they had never heard of Arochuku nor many of the towns through which the soldiers had to make their way.

Not so Mary, however. While unwillingly marking time at Akpap, she had plotted her future advance and made persistent inquiries of the people who were coming from greater and greater distances to seek her services, even from Ibo and Ibibio country.

She had also learned a good deal from the Aro slave dealers who passed through Okoyong. Helpless to impress them with a sense of their own wrongdoing, she would shake her fist at them as they went by; but she nursed them in illness and sorted out their palavers as she did with everyone else. When she tried to persuade them of the viciousness of their calling they would laugh and shrug and dare her to come and teach them better, taken aback when she swore she would do just that the moment she had someone to take her place.

Mary being what she was, no place attracted her more than Arochuku itself. She longed to confront the dreaded priests and denizens of that grisly grotto, as she did the menacing Egbo men, to tear away their fearsome apparatus and defy them to harm her. She was told she would be killed, but she was not so alarmed as she had once been by the savagery each tribe attributed to its neighbour. They would see, she told the slavers, she would come.

She renewed her pleas to the Mission to send up two women to hold Okoyong while she investigated the possibilities beyond. But soldiers would confront Chuku before she could. In August, 1901, as the dry season approached, the government began to establish forward bases at Itu and further up the river at Unwana, and all missionaries were ordered down to Calabar.

None wanted to leave their station at a time when the people were unsettled by the mass movement of troops, and Mary protested with characteristic vehemence: "My people won't fight!" But the government would not risk a white missionary being kidnapped for a hostage. A military escort, courteous but adamant, arrived by launch to fetch her and her household, and down to civilisation, for the first time in three years, they went.

Mary came up out of the bush into the atmosphere of the town now like a water creature surfacing briefly and scuttling back into its own milieu at the first opportunity. She complained of the "terrible bright sky". The Governor, mindful of what his administration owed to this strange, determined woman, proposed building her a house. But Mary chose to settle into a room in the European Hospital, which was neither comfortable nor private, and work behind the scenes. For many up-river chiefs, perplexed by events, were coming to seek her advice.

Calabar had become a military encampment. There were several thousand African troops with hundreds more carriers and 150 European officers. Everyone turned out to watch as the contingents of soldiers embarked. For the children from the house in lonely Akpap it must have been immeasurably exciting.

The missionaries generally approved of the expedition but maintained that, had the home Church backed them up with money and manpower to open up the west bank of the river, no columns of soldiers would have been necessary. "But," said Mary, "since the sword and gun are before us, we must follow at once."

Sword and gun quickly achieved their end. While two columns converged on Arochuku by land, the main force travelled up the Enyong Creek in steel canoes. The Aros drummed out a call for help wherever their influence reached but, in the erroneous belief that the white-skinned enemy were albinos, and therefore unable to see by day, advanced recklessly against much superior forces and were easily overcome. By Christmas Eve 1901, the expeditionary force was reunited on the edge of Arochuku, about a mile from the sacred grove. All that remained of the Oracle's long history were a few gruesome relics, a starved goat awaiting sacrifice, a newly severed head. On the last day of the year the soldiers dynamited the ravine. Some priests escaped, and with them some of the Oracle's mystery, so that even today the Long Juju is not totally extinct; but the obliteration of the shrine marked the end of its temporal power. By March, units of soldiers were fanning out to fill the administrative vacuum left by the discredited priests in the main centres of population.

Once the news reached Calabar that Arochuku was taken, Mary made off home without awaiting official permission. Neither she nor the children had been well in the three months they had spent in the town. Probably it was as Dan Slessor has said—if she could not work she would be ill.

During the early months of the year she lent her prestige to efforts to negotiate a settlement. Sir Ralph Moor travelled up to hold palaver with chiefs, many of whom had never seen a white man, and messengers came running to Mary for advice—what to do, what to say. It has been said that it was largely thanks to her influence that equitable terms were agreed.

All this intensified her interest in the west bank of the river. It was no hit-and-miss infatuation with the unknown. The conviction was growing on her that the Enyong Creek was a strategic roadway to the interior. On its southern bank were the Ibibios, on its north the Ibos, at its source the high country of Bende leading on to no one yet knew where. And at a focal point on the Cross River, high up, stood Itu, the age-old slave market, commanding both river and creek.

Mary's time in Calabar had proved interesting. She had been

able to compare notes with missionaries gathered in from all the out-stations and pick the brains of those officials who had to do with the new regions. She had also managed to transmit her own enthusiasm to some of the young newcomers, so far held back by the caution of the Mission Board. One, a young teacher with four years' experience, called Janet Wright, volunteered to move up and hold Akpap so that Mary could move on.

She also had the satisfaction of seeing her brainchild of nine years earlier, the industrial training school called the Hope Waddell Institute, a flourishing concern with facilities for both boys and girls.

But Mary was in the grip of a single vision — to press forward — and Itu became her first objective. Alexander Cruickshank had started a school there in the same year that Roger Casement was driven off by the Aros, but had met crushing opposition over the question of admitting twins. Recently, however, the chiefs of the town, threatened with attack by some Calabar traders, had begun to see certain advantages in having a white missionary working in their midst and, collecting some money, they took it to Mary asking to "buy the word of God". For her this was springboard enough.

In January, leaving Jean in charge, she travelled up the river to Itu by canoe, taking with her three of the young people she had trained, two boys and Mana, a slave girl. She found the high posi-tion of the town as fine as that of Calabar. The chiefs allowed her to choose a site on the hill for her church and school. Mary marked out the plan for the church, with two rooms at the end for her own use, and worked beside the people as they began building. She was much struck by the comparative freedom and independence of the women — "sparks of wit and satire . . . flew with as much zest as ever obtained in a Galloway byre or market fairin'. It is such a treat for me, for no intercourse is permitted between the sexes in Oko-yong, except that of the family, and then it is strained and unnatural, but here they were daffin' and lauchin' as in Scotland."

She settled her young folk among the people with justifiable con-fidence and left for Akpap among cries of, "Don't be long in coming back, Ma!" and leading by a string the goat her new friends had given her.

She had no Mission authorisation for this start, but — and this was at the crux of her increasing independence — neither had she spent any Mission money. The youngsters, inspired by her own zeal, worked for their keep alone, and this was provided by the townspeople.

Mary visited them frequently and felt that so modest a beginning was amply justified.

It was some months before Janet Wright was officially posted to Akpap but when at last she arrived, she lived up to every expectation. Besides teaching, she had practical experience of nursing and dress-making, and was splendid with the children. "She is a right sisterly helpmate, a real help and comfort in every way," wrote Mary.

Several courses were now open to her. She had corresponded with the government medical officer, Dr. Adam, at Bende, and learned that the population was not so large as had been thought and that the Church Missionary Society, long active on the Niger River side of Iboland, was thinking of taking up work there. The Anglicans and Presbyterians tried not to tread on one another's toes, but there were no such cordial relations with the Roman Catholics. In fact, suspicion that "that corrupt body" intended moving into Bende had precisely the effect of rousing Mary's fighting spirit. "Oh, if I were able to go or send even a few of my bairns just to take hold!" But she did not feel sure God wanted her to go there.

Just to take hold! became Mary's constant refrain. The conviction was growing on her that even the slightest contact undertaken in the right spirit could be the beginning of new life. If she had not someone with *ten* Bible lessons behind him to send, she would prefer to send someone with only *five* rather than refuse the overtures that were being made to her. But she still did not know in which direction to turn, and was certain that when the time was ripe, she *would* know. In her Bible, against the words ". . . and the voice of the Lord came unto him" (Moses) she wrote, "He was quite sure. God gives a *voice* when He wishes us to hear."

In June, Mary set off with a couple of her boys to try and catch the government launch on its weekly trip to Itu. The launch was not in sight when she reached Ikunetu village and, leaving the lads to watch for it, she rested from her six mile walk in the local teacher's house. On hearing the slow throb of engines, she rushed outside to find that the launch was already passing and it was too late to hail it. There was nothing for it but to toil back again to Akpap. Miss Wright was full of commiseration over this misfortune, knowing Mary had no strength to waste, but Mary did not fret. "Och, lassie," she said, "God dinna intend me to go today."

What He did intend was, she believed, made clear the following week when she found herself aboard the launch in company with the Aro expedition's commander, Lt. Colonel Montanaro, who was on his way to Arochuku. In reply to her eager questions about the state of the people there, he pressed her to continue the journey and see for herself.

Mary had made no provision for a stay among strangers, nor had she anything like permission to begin work in the Calabar Mission's name in a totally new place. But, convinced that God was leading, she agreed to go on, though she was without food or so much as a change of clothing.

Leaving the steel canoe at Amasu, on the bank of the Enyong Creek, she walked the four miles to Arochuku, surprised by the teeming population of the area. Even now she could not help feeling a certain trepidation as she approached a place of such dark notoriety. But eighteen months of military rule had suppressed all outward signs of past excesses. Skulls and totems no longer trimmed the doorposts and the grotto of the Long Juju appeared totally unremarkable, with the ruined altars grown over, green and still. One busy village ran straight into the next until the country opened out wide and beautiful towards the hills of Bende. The people appeared very friendly.

Her old acquaintances, the slave dealers, hailed her on the track with "Welcome, Ma!" and declared they had been expecting her. Deprived of their ancient livelihood, they were turning over the possibilities of legitimate trade and were eager to "learn book". Already she found people anxious to emulate the coastal towns in setting up churches and schools. The chiefs she gathered together seemed delighted that she should start work at Amasu.

It was a canoe journey of at least five hours between Amasu and Itu, even when the river was high enough to get all the way by water, but within the month Mary had gone home to Akpap and fetched two of her boys back to take charge of a school at Amasu. As in the early days at Ekenge there was much initial enthusiasm.

Her journey down the creek this time was marked by a striking incident which Mary described in a July letter to the *Record*:

. . . a small canoe shot out from behind a clump of bushes and struck itself on our larger craft. I apologised to the man, and he immediately said, with cap in hand "I meant it, Ma; I have been waiting for you," and he took a book from his cap and handed it to me. The boys were for going on; but he said, "My master begged me to waylay you and bring you to his house. The boys know where it is, and it will not take you much off your road." I read the letter [in said book]. We turned the boat's head and glided into

God + One, are always a majority.

God's secure protection. **PSALMS 4-6.**

sands of people, that have set *them-selves* against me round about.

7 Arise, O LORD; save me, O my

5 The fool... sight: thou ... quity.

A page from one of Mary Slessor's Bibles

The black and white Dans, 1907

such a lake of aquatic plants and flowers as I believe could not be surpassed anywhere ... On we ran as in an extravagant dream, till we struck a shingly beach, and found, among the crowd of canoes, large oil boats, and all the etcetera of a busy trading place, a fine looking, well-dressed young man and a very handsome well-dressed woman, and welcoming hands stretched out to assist us in landing.

He led us to a pretty little room with concrete floor, a European bedstead, clean and dainty, with mosquito curtains, and all the etcetera of a man of taste. I asked him why he had sent for us, and then in a manly way he told his very touching story. His house had once been burned, and he was cursing the witchcraft which had caused it, when a Duke Town man told him the Bible way of looking at things, and prayed for and with him. From that time he had had thoughts of God and doubts of his old heathen beliefs — but he never took a step to find out more, till lately his only child died. Then he vowed he would seek God, and though the town people laughed, and then moved off from him, he was determined to go on and be delivered from the slavery and darkness of his doubt.

So he went and watched for me at Itu, as he did not know Okoyong. The first time I was away when he reached Itu, but he found an old teacher of Creek Town who had been a besotted drunkard, without a home, for over a decade; still, he [the chief] engaged him to come and read the Bible to him, for his old friend was dead. When he sent to Itu again, on hearing I was there, he found me gone to Amasu; so he kept a man there watching for my return. And now would I deliver him, and show him what to do. By this time several big, fattened ladies were come in, and lots of dependents and children. I said we had better pray before we went further. Then I got the drunken teacher's Bible, and read from it all the passages which occurred to me, and tried to show him the way of salvation. To make a long story short, I wrote an order to Mr. Addison for ABC cards, books, slates, etc. and told them I would send or come very soon to see that this teacher began to teach them all to read, so that they might have the Word of God to guide them.

You can guess the set-off we got, and though we got a storm of wind and rain for our delay, the boys pulled with a will, and my heart kept singing and praying till we got to Itu, where the joy was shared by my boys *there*, and their pupils, old and young.

Between the thoughtful young Chief Onoyom Iya Nya and the

besotted teacher, Christianity flourished in Akani Obio. When the first church he built was washed away by floods and his people quaked under the seeming vengeance of the old gods, the chief had faith enough, with Mary's encouragement, to build not only a new church but a whole new village on higher ground. His conversion, Mary wrote, "created a sensation everywhere".

In August, at the end of fifteen years in Okoyong, Mary saw her work reach quiet culmination in the first communion service to be held there. It is startling to realise that, for all the changes that had come about, in fifteen years not a single person had been baptised. Even then, of the dozen expected to join the Church, five were persuaded at the last moment by anxious relatives to withdraw, at least until they had had the chance to see the effect of this strange *mbiam* on the seven brave souls that remained. It is perhaps unkind to suggest that it may have been the expectation of some attendant cataclysm that swelled the watching congregation to 213 people.

Seven of the eleven children baptised were Mary's own. She had lately acquired the last two babies, Asuquo, a boy of Efik extraction, and the girl twin she called Madge White ("Whitie"). This made eight children who had no other home but hers. Jean had been christened long years before in Dundee, but the rest—Annie, Alice, Mary, Maggie, Dan, Whitie and Asuquo—were baptised that day. Of the communicants, too, more than half were of Mary's inner circle—Jean, the faithful Iye, Mana and her fellow teacher at Itu, Esien.

After it was all over, the minister who had taken the service, wrote: "Miss Slessor has had to wait a long time for the first actual gathering into the visible church." But, for Mary, aware of the complete break with family and society which Christian witness involved, this small showing was a proud one.

This day also marked the end of her first pioneering period. Now she was to leave all she had achieved behind her and start again.

13

SQUARE PEG

THE GREATEST OPPORTUNITIES seemed to offer themselves just
as Mary's five-year tour was drawing to an end. She was due to go
on furlough in January 1904, but the pull of the newly opened
waterways was strong upon her. The Ibo and Ibibio lands were in
ferment, wide open to forceful leadership. The people, bewildered
by the changes that had taken place and by the presence of soldiers
in their midst, looked to the missionaries to help them make a transition to the new order. They begged for teachers.

But the home Church had forbidden further expansion. Rather
than bow meekly to this ban, Mary, in a wonderfully lucid letter to
the Committee in Calabar, proposed a whole new way of working:

> . . . something more mobile and flexible than ordinary congrega-
> tional work and methods. The scattered broken units into which
> our African populations are divided, their various *jujus* and
> *mbiams* and superstitions which segregate even the houses of any
> common village, make it necessary for us to do more than merely
> pay an occasional visit, even if that visit results in a church or a
> school being built.

She suggested that bands of Church members might travel and
teach in their own neighbourhoods, that Christian traders could be
encouraged to give Bible instruction on their visits to up-river
stations and so "a chain of personal interest and living sympathy
link on the raw heathen to the church centres . . . without the
material expense which the opening of new stations involves."

She declared categorically that she had not the slightest intention
of going to Britain – "I am thankful to say I do not feel any necessity
for so doing" – but proposed to use the year she would normally
have spent on leave in building up the work along the Enyong
Creek.

> I have visited several towns of Enyong in the Creek, and have
> found good enough accommodation as there are semi-European

houses available and open for a lodging. I shall find my own canoe and crew, and shall stay at any given place any length of time which the circumstances suggest, so as not to tax my own strength, and members of my own family shall help in the elementary teaching in the schools.

What she really wanted was an ordained minister and his wife to take over Okoyong so that Miss Wright might establish a base for them both at Itu.

. . . as a natural and strategic point in the business conduct of our Mission, Itu is incomparable. It was not without reason that it was the slave mart, and that it became the government base for all work, both for north and flank. The gateway to the Aros and Ibibios, holding the Enyong, and being just a day's journey from what must ever be our base, namely the seaport of the ocean steamers, having waterway all the year round and a good beach front, it is the natural point, I think, at which our up and down river work should converge.

The Committee, when it met in November, considered that she had made an incontestable case for Itu, and decided to build a medical station there. But Mary's plan to devote her year of rest and recuperation to the most strenuous sort of pioneering work was so unprecented that it had to be referred to Edinburgh for a decision.

They knew Mary had made up her mind and would be obstinate. Yet health was the crux of the matter, as desperate a problem as it had ever been. Apart from those many like Charles Morrison who were invalided home never to return—a fate Mary herself narrowly escaped—the roll of the dead mounted yearly. Recently there had been Alexander Cruickshank's wife; John Bishop, the printer who had accompanied Mary to Okoyong; the engineer of the river steamer, who took mail and news to the out-stations; a young nurse only two months in the country. All died of blackwater, typhoid or haematuric fever. The likelihood of "succumbing" to the climate was ever in people's minds.

Mary's strength was not great, whatever her protestations. Before the Committee met in April she suffered a serious illness and rose "a mere wreck of what I was . . . nervous and easily knocked up, and so rheumatic that I cannot get up or down without pain." But it was useless to pretend that with Miss Slessor ordinary rules applied. While offering every inducement to her to go home, promising to make arrangements both for her work and for her children if she did so, the Committee bowed to the inevitable and gave permission for her to proceed as she thought fit.

Two young women went up to relieve Akpap and while Jean — who, was, Mary said, her right hand and her left — assumed responsibility for the family, Mary prepared for her roving commission.

She was sworn not to commit the Mission to any expense whatever, not even to the equivalent cost of her own passage home. She would have to support her family and helpers, hire canoes, maintain those pupils she had settled at out-stations and equip all her new work out of a salary of a hundred pounds a year — less than two pounds a week. But she refused to worry about money. Fortunately she had many friends personally interested in her work who were generous with gifts. The indigenous foods — yams and beans and cassava, palm oil and chickens, eggs and fish — were cheap and easily procured. And Africans rarely accept services without returning something in kind — probably much of their food was given them.

Mary went down to Duke Town for the first time since her evacuation there in 1901 and resigned her post as government agent, which she had kept up for twelve years. She laid in stores and, out of her small hoard, bought "building materials" for the schools and churches she hoped to leave in her wake. Probably these were no more than hinges and locks, cement for floors and a few sawn timbers for furniture, since the buildings would be of local materials.

In July 1904, she moved her family to Itu, confessing mild misgivings at the thought of starting a "gypsy life in a canoe" with a family of seven children. There she stayed for a time. A government doctor found her "in a native hut with a few of the barest necessities of furniture . . . rocking a tiny baby while five others were quietly sleeping wrapped up in bits of brown paper and newspaper in other parts of the room", and marvelled that she could look after them all and still do the "colossal" work she did.

She was fifty-five and becoming time-worn. The thinning hair, no longer cut in a boyish "bob" but twisted into a skinny topknot, had not so much of the "fire" about it; but her body was erect and sprung for action and the blue eyes sparkled with impish humour. She had fought tooth and nail for the privilege of planting Christianity in the new regions, yet remained sublimely innocent of any personal claim upon them. "Whether I shall find His place for me up-river or whether I shall come back to my own people again, I do not know. He knows and that is enough."

Her own people were not easily reconciled to losing her — "They

seem to think no-one can settle their affairs but this old lady"—
and sent deputations to recall her:

> . . . as I was reading over again the letters in the quiet, a blaze of
> light shone over the top of the door—the house is not nearly
> finished yet—and here were fifteen young men from Olroyoro
> [Okoyong] who were perplexed as to what they should do, seeing
> that the ladies who had come only a month ago to relieve me for
> this work had already gone and left them without a teacher.

They came from other parts too, asking her for teachers, for
books—even for God!

Her own account of these months gives some notion of her
methods but little of the physical difficulties and personal opposition
encountered.

> . . . as it was a very wet season and the water was fearfully high
> and strong, I did not attempt much *direct* visitation work, but
> tried to develop Itu and make our houses fit, so that in the dry
> season we should be able to devote our whole time to going about.
> So we took charge of the Creek stations more by proxy and
> management than by personal visitation. Meanwhile boys were
> teaching in the schools, and any Efik trader who could read and
> knew the Gospel helped in a Sabbath service; and without these
> they prayed and sang and exhorted among themselves . . .

This picture of the almost totally uninstructed trying to help one
another is reminiscent of St. Paul's description of some of the early
Christian churches.

In September she wrote:

> I am writing this in my shed at Amasu, in Inokon. The boys are
> putting in the long big sticks which make the walls. The ants and
> damp have made ducks and drakes of the place, but with a new
> wall I shall be able to stay in it on my next visit, which will be
> probably about a month hence.

She moved as the spirit led her. One day when she had lost her
way,

> . . . two men took charge of my bundles and bairns and led me to a
> bridge round a little way. Then one asked me if I had come with
> God's word. What else should I come with, I replied. "Oh," he
> said, "We have built a small church, and are longing for you to
> come, and teach us, and we will build a house for you to stay in."
> But I could not let the chance of the boat slip. I shall, however, go

back and stay a little time with them next month, and build.

In November the Calabar Committee met to hear Mary's account of her months of wandering and were deeply impressed. While reiterating with true Scottish caution their stipulation against committing either men or funds in her further endeavours, they extended her roving commission for another six months. She had vividly demonstrated what could be done with next to nothing in the way of resources.

If her fellow missionaries had been chary in their praises in the past, they were not so now, particularly the younger men. Mr. Macgregor, Principal of the Hope Waddell Institute, found her "no ordinary woman". Mr. Wilkie firmly declared that had she been able to undertake this work earlier it is doubtful whether the Aro expedition would have been necessary. Mr. Luke wrote: "Where the Church has failed a single woman has stepped into the breach." In an eloquent appeal for reinforcements he compared her work to "scattering a pinch of crumbs before a starving multitude".

But she was an uncomfortable team-mate, for she demanded a whole new approach which laid little stress on those firm educational foundations and solid permanent buildings so dear to the hearts of most. Her teaching was off-hand and sporadic. She was always on the move, difficult to find, and *would not* take care of herself.

She was also tolerant where many of her fellows were uncompromising. She had scant patience with Protestant-Catholic rivalry in the mission field, declaring, "They'll nae take them tae Hell!" All the same, she implored her own Church not to let slip their prior right to work along the Cross River:

> It is time we were bestirring ourselves to choose a site or sites for the taking hold of these hordes of people, else the Roman Catholics will be before us, or any one the government may find willing to guide and teach the natives. And justly too, as we have no right by reason of our past history to keep out those who, but for us, would take the word of life to these peoples.

And of Arochuku she wrote:

> My object in going was twofold. First, it was the fulfilment of and old promise to those slave traders; and second, it was capturing the base of the Aro country, and thus keeping an open door for Protestant gospel truth without our ever incurring the blame of transgressing the principals of Christian comity.

One of her unshakeable convictions was in direct opposition to the thoughts of the Mission at large, and that was that the pioneer work was best done by women. She urged that even African men declared "Ma, we don't want a man; we want a woman like you to come and teach our girls to read, and sew, and wash, and know God's book." "Women can do the spadework best," she wrote.

While Mary returned to the Creek stations the Mission authorities began to give shape to one of her most cherished dreams, the building of a medical station at Itu. It was to consist initially of a simple, sixteen-bed hospital, with an operating theatre and dispensary, and a launch so that the doctor could visit outlying dispensaries. Dr. David Robertson of Calabar was to be in charge.

"It seems like a fairy tale," wrote Mary. "I don't know what to say. I can just look into the blue sky and say 'Even so, Father; in good and ill, let me live and be worthy of it all.' It's a grand gift and I am so glad for my people."

Meanwhile she was giving her attention to the Ibibios, those oppressed clans squeezed between the slave-dealing Aros and the no less predatory coastal traders:

> They are the food and oil producers [she wrote in the *Record*] and they have been so numerous that they have been the happy hunting ground for slaves, and the down-trodden of Calabar and of all the middle men tribes. They were bought for half the prices of the Aros, and hence they are sulky, deceitful and in every sense inferior. They are nevertheless the workers; alert, lithe, silent, they glide past every one as quickly as they can, as if in fear. But they can be won . . .

Their claims were pressed upon her by Charles Partridge, the District Commissioner at Ikot Ekpene, the new military and administrative centre twenty-five miles from Itu. Arriving in December 1904, he ingratiated himself at once with the gift of a Christmas pudding, the first Mary had tasted in years. She responded with neighbourly offers of help.

Charles Partridge was a man of the soldier-scholar breed, a dreamer in action. Now thirty-three, he had studied theology at Cambridge and then veered off into the comparatively new discipline of anthropology, so that his sympathy with the "bush" Africans was unusually well-informed. A Fellow of the Royal Geographical Society, he was also an enthusiastic photographer and, out of his previous tour up-river, had compiled a fine book of photographs and commentary, *Cross River Natives*, as yet unpublished and unknown to Mary.

At his instigation, Mary explored the country between Itu and Ikot Ekpene, which were fast being linked by road, and took options on land at Ikot Obong and Use Ikot Oku, about six miles from Itu and two miles apart. In May 1905 she wrote:

> I have thought of beginning my project for a farm school so as to help any handicapped woman or twin to a livelihood, while under gospel teaching, and having a shelter in a Mission house. Of late this claim has come so close to my very door that probably before this month [May] is over I shall have committed myself to something definite here, too. This is the best centre by which the maximum of good can be got from the minimum of expenditure. The expenditure of money is not in question. I am guarded against this by the express command of the Committee. I shall only expend my own, or what my personal friends give me. I mean principally the expenditure of labour, and strength, and time, so as to safeguard the lives of our workers. In this I shall follow the lines of transport, and help, and high land.

A month later she had moved to Ikot Obong and even agreed to assume the work of vice-president of the native court—a new name for her old function, though now she came under the District Commissioner. Through the court she could fight abuses and institute reforms more swiftly than through services and classes, for court sessions were always well-attended and she had power both to reprove and punish. It also brought a wider range of people within reach of her influence. At Ikot Obong, in those early days, the court occupied a great deal of her time.

Soon she had a "bush" house built in which she could settle down with her family after a year of camping about. To do so, however, was an act of some effrontery, for technically she was still on leave from Akpap, with no authority whatever to man a new station on anything like a permanent basis. Her mind was set, however, and nothing would make her go back. The distress of their departure from Okoyong has been described by Dan Slessor, who was six at the time:

> It was a most pathetic morning; wailing rent the air, you cannot imagine a whole people so stricken and distressed; swarms of them came from distant villages afar, with all sorts of presents including yams, plantains, goats, chickens, eggs—so plentiful that if all were accepted there would be no room in the Mission launch, "Jubilee". I had no tears to shed. My brother and sister

of the same womb were weeping profusely; my remote relatives were half in tears, half wondering if they would ever see Etim [my native name] again. The Obong and Elders comforted them. "Ma will take good care of him for us." At Ikunetu, as the launch moved off for Itu, the great wail went up like thunder, men and women weeping. Ma stood on the upper deck, waving emotionally, but her thoughts remained in the Mission house far away up the hill. As the launch turned the bend, she collapsed into her arm-chair, "Oh my people, my people, my friends!"

At such moments no one dared disturb her. The older girls knew already that during such moments Ma was not with them . . . At length Ma would come to, her eyes red and filled with tears; without another word, she would move gently towards the canteen box, open it, bring up loaves of bread, butter, some cheese, other provisions and tea. Jane would get up heavily to help, but Ma would say kindly, "Sit down, Jane; it is my duty to serve you all; I have brought you away from your homes." Out would come the cups and tea goes round.

Mary's first year among the Ibibios was productive. She enjoyed a rare sense of comradeship with the District Commissioner who was, in the area of her court work, and by courtesy at least, her "boss". Together they tramped through the bush seeking suitable vantage points for Mary's future work. Though their meetings were infrequent and their houses many miles apart, they exchanged books and papers and friendly letters by the government messengers who went to and fro.

The political officers played a larger and larger part in Mary's life. Like her, they were on the move. Naturally disposed to look kindly on the young and adventurous, she became devoted to many of them, although, as she was also fiercely opinionated and did not suffer fools gladly, they had to watch their step with her.

How Mary combined political authority with deep compassion shows in a passage from a letter of October 1905.

My new room is crowded with a savage lot of men and women. A murder has been perpetrated close by, about a woman. She is but a girl, and they have brought her here in preference to tying her up and torturing her to confess whom she wants for her husband, seeing she declares she will never marry this one to whom she has been betrothed from infancy. She has invented several excuses, the chief one being that there is one of his wives whom she does not like. God help these poor down-trodden women! The constant cause of palaver and bloodshed here is marriage. It is a dreadful state of society. I have left them a little, to see whether she will confess. If she will not, I cannot give her over to them; the safer way is to keep her as a prisoner on parole, and get a place for her to sleep with some woman near. The two policemen are away to see to the murdered man.

One object of her crusade at Ikot Obong was the large encampment of road labourers — several hundred of them recruited from a wide area. Their European supervisors made friendly neighbours for a time.

At the New Year, Janet Wright and a new colleague, Mina Amess, paid Mary a visit from Akpap, and not far short of Ikot Obong were hailed by three surveyors who invited them to dinner at their camp. "Ma won't have anything in the house," they declared, and insisted on sending a message asking her to join them, and to come dressed as she was. Mary arrived in her dressing-gown, and the six sat down to table. But informality had its limits. As the men made to start their soup she stayed them with a firm gesture. "No ye don't, laddies. We'll hae a blessing first!"

The gallantry of the lonely men made for a little light relief in the strenuous lives of these women. And how much the presence of an amusing, warm-hearted white woman could mean to them was shown by the fact that at Christmas eight normally hard-drinking fellows welcomed the chance to spend the whole day with Mary, contributing whatever they had of Christmas fare and much of merriment, but, in deference to her, touching not a drop of alcohol.

Mr. Partridge had enticed Mary to come to Ikot Obong with the promise that there would soon be good roads. But Mary could hardly believe the speed with which the road gangs pushed their way through "solitary wilderness of the most forbidding description, where the silence of the bush had never been broken." There, where the wheel itself was hitherto unknown and no beast of burden could survive the assaults of the tsetse-fly, she was thrilled to see young officials go speeding past on bicycles. Charles Partridge, correctly gauging her mettle, presented her with one of her own, and her passion for distance made learning to ride an easy matter, even at fifty-six and in a state of very indifferent health!

The new road makes it easy to ride and I'm running up and down and taking a new bit in a village two miles off. It has done me all the good in the world, and I will soon be able to overtake more work. I wonder what the Andersons and the Goldies and the

Edgerleys will say when they see that we can cycle twenty miles in the bush!

Another new marvel produced by Partridge was a phonograph, and Mary was equally quick to grasp at its possibilities. Together they held an impromptu Sunday night service in the Ikot Obong court house, accompanying Scriptural lantern slides with records of familiar hymns.

. . . I spoke into the "trumpet" the parable of the Prodigal [Luke XV]; and it was reproduced twice over in a trumpet tone. The audience was simply electrified. That parable has gone on to be reproduced all over the Ibibio towns where our Administrator will be going on his civilising and governing tours. Is it not grand? . . . A person with means could get the Gospel carried round like that when he or she could not speak a word of the language.

As the Itu hospital was near completion, one benefactor offered to foot most of the bill and at the same time suggested the name "Mary Slessor Mission Hospital". Mary was overcome. "I feel as if I can never come out of the bush and go among other people with this distinguishing mark on me . . . I've not sacrificed a single happiness or incurred a single hardship by my work, for I have such an even, happy peaceful, satisfied life that I feel quite a fraud . . ."

Nevertheless, she was in rebellious mood. A reminder had come to her from the Women's Foreign Mission Committee that her leave of absence from her post at Akpap was now up and she should return forthwith.

Mary did not even consider complying. "Whether the Church permits it or not, I feel I must stay here, and even go on further, as roads are made." To Partridge she wrote that she would simply refuse to go back. She felt disenchanted with the ponderous methods of the Church and declared she would not mind "cutting the rope and going adrift" with her children, if necessary.

This was not mere obstinacy. In a deeply telling letter to the *Women's Missionary Magazine* (the italics are ours), she explained:

I have been thinking much about the Christian's armour, and the shoes have come home to me more than ever before. Just now, *I am the feet of the Church, as it were, and I am to go with shoes of peace*. What a preparation for the government that is — to pave the transition road with Gospel peace!

But it was a question how often she could flout authority. She was prepared, if her intransigence brought about her dismissal, to support herself by trade or even by accepting from the government the salary she had lately refused. Too often she had found herself a square peg in a round hole, at loggerheads with her colleagues. The conflict between the concentration of work in one area and what is nowadays called "outreach" had never been resolved.

The Mission, however, had no wish for a head-on collision with one whose following was as great as Mary's. Again they gave way, but firmly stipulated that in *future* the Women's Foreign Mission should not lead but follow — a rule that in Mary's case was only made to be broken.

Mina Amess joined Mary at Ikot Obong in the spring, when Janet Wright went home on leave. She had been much warned of the older woman's austerities and arrived heavily laden with water filter, mosquito net and all the camp kit she needed to keep house alongside one who would have none of these things. She dreaded to hear what Mary, with her caustic tongue, would say to her *sixteen* head-loads of equipment. But Mary only cast a wry glance at it all and remarked: "Ye mauna hae yer filters nowadays. Filters werna created; they were an afterthought!"

The two got on well. Miss Amess was pleasant company and an excellent cook, particularly of home treats like steamed pudding. Mary greatly appreciated an invitation to supper with her after a long day in court or on mail nights when they had news to share with one another.

For the younger woman life with Mary was full of surprises. She once woke to strange noises in the middle of the night and found Mary building a fireplace. Yet, in the daytime, if she reminded Mary that it was schooltime when they were engaged together in something Mary enjoyed — she loved reading aloud the novels of Ouida — Mary would say "Dinna worry about that, just keep them in at the other end!"

It was Mina Amess who inherited Mary's station at Akpap and — a good linguist and efficient administrator — carried on the work for thirty-three years. She moved there in 1907 as Mary prepared to go on her long-overdue furlough.

14

THE COURT WHERE NO WOMAN
LOST A CASE

FOR MOST OF fifteen years now Mary had assumed, along with her other preoccupations, a considerable load of official court work which has been mentioned only in passing. It deserves amplification.

Her appointment as Vice-Consul in 1892, when the Protectorate was just beginning to extend its sway, showed radical good sense on the part of the government, for the people of Okoyong had already, in effect, made Mary their judge and intercessor. Still, Governor Macdonald displayed surprising foresight in making that state of affairs official. She was, after all, not only a missionary, but a *woman*. And the terms of her appointment gave her power to conduct most of the tribe's affairs, including presiding over its courts.

She was not the only missionary to be given jurisdiction over a native court in Calabar Province, for one of the problems of early administration in this area was the absence of powerful and generally trusted chiefs. Many so-called chiefs were little more than heads of households, prone to perpetuate age-old bickerings with their neighbours. Nor were such men literate. The comparative impartiality of a foreigner with good local knowledge, able to oversee the activities of court clerks and messengers, made him a useful link, at this crucial stage, between government and people.

But the choice of a woman was another matter. In 1892 it was totally unprecedented. One can imagine heads wagging in disapproval in Calabar, faraway Whitehall, and still more distant Scotland. If a woman *could* act the part of a Solomon, *should* she? Was it proper that a Christian woman should give ear to all the sordid palavers of the tribe? Many missionaries thought not.

Painful as might be the shocks to her delicate feminine sensibilities, there is no evidence that Mary was disinclined to accept the post. In this, as in so much else, she was a pioneer. For it was not until after the passing of the oddly named statute, "The Sex Disqualification Removal Act" of 1919, that the first woman magistrate came to be appointed in England. In Nigeria the first African woman magistrate, barrister Stella Thomas, was appointed only in 1942.

It is hard to know how much her new official status altered Mary's working life. The court work was an added responsibility, of course. The long sittings, the marches from one village to another, took a toll of her strength, while her heart often ached at the sufferings and raw cruelty that were exposed. She continued, however, to be guided more by her own conscience than by law. The Police Magistrate at Calabar, T. D. Maxwell, later Justice of the Supreme Court, described with a touch of envy the freedom with which she used her powers:

> One decision I recall—I have often subsequently wished that I could follow it as a precedent. A sued B for a small debt. B admitted owing the money and the Court [that is, "Ma"] ordered him to pay accordingly: but she added, "A is a rascal. He treats his mother shamefully, he neglects his children, only the other day he beat one of his wives with quite unnecessary vehemence, yes and she was B's sister too, his farm is a disgrace, he seldom washes, and then there was the palaver about C's goat a month ago. Oh, of course A didn't steal it, he was found not guilty, wasn't he?—all the same the affair was never satisfactorily cleared up, and he did look unusually sleek just about then. On the other hand, B was thrifty and respectable, so before B paid the amount due he would give A good sound caning in the presence of everybody."

Mr. Maxwell added that no court he had attended seemed to him so well to deserve the name "Court of Justice".

When Mary settled at Ikot Obong in 1905, she was invited by the High Commissioner to become permanent Vice-President of Itu native court, presiding member of a panel of local elders. Court seems to have been held two days a week, though in view of her constant travelling this must have been somewhat elastic. To her also fell the job of recording the evidence and judgment. Some of her record books have survived. Professor Jeffreys relates* how he searched for and finally unearthed them "mouldering away in an outbuilding of the Government Rest House". Later, the records were collected and bound. But the African climate is unkind to documents. When studied by one of the present authors in 1948, the red leather covers of the book and the first pages were mildewed and worm-eaten, and the ink badly faded.

* In *The West African Revue*, June, 1950.

All the judgments were written by Mary in her own hand and initialled, but not always signed. The language seems curious until one remembers that she was trying the case in Ibibio, attempting to wrest the truth from reluctant witnesses in their own tongue at the same time as she set it all down in English.

The cases cover a wide field—lands, debts, contempt of court, defamation of character, wife-stealing, child-stealing, adultery. In the background of most of the cases is the dread of witchcraft. Plaintiffs constantly assert that curses have been laid on them, on their houses, on their wives.

In Okoyong Mary probably held court on the verandah of whatever place she was staying, or in a local palaver house. A photograph shows her seated just outside a simple palm-leaf shelter, in a basketwork chair before a small three-legged table on which she could write. The three chiefs who, with her, constituted the court sit around her, while the court messenger in brass-buttoned uniform stands stiffly behind. Before her would be the interested parties and a crowd of onlookers, for then, as now, the court provided a fascinating free form of entertainment.

At Ikot Obong, where there was a long, low mud-and-thatch court house and such refinements as a bamboo-screened "retiring" room where the court could consider its verdict, the proceedings may have been marginally more formal than at Okoyong. None of the surviving judgments, certainly, is quite so untrammelled as the one cited earlier. There was still, however, plenty of scope for application of private knowledge, the insight that only a close familiarity with day-to-day affairs and gossip can give.

There were at this time three kinds of court in the Protectorate —the Supreme Court, where the most serious cases were tried, the District Court, presided over by the District Commissioner, which dealt with civil cases and charges of petty larceny and assault, and the Native Court, where, as far as possible, judgment was given in accordance with local custom.

Not all of Mary's fellow missionaries would have felt able to associate themselves with the "customary" courts. By accepting local codes to such an extent they could be said to entrench many of those customs the Church was bound to oppose. Mary did not hesitate to bend the court to effect changes of custom where she could. But it may be wondered how more doctrinaire Christians, visiting her court sessions, reacted to the swearing-in of witnesses on the native *mbiam*—or the spectacle of Mary bringing a difficult case to an end by ordering the opposing parties to *chop mbiam* in an

Mary's household and guest, about 1911

Daniel Slessor and his daughters lay a wreath on Mary Slessor's grave 1965

A street in Calabar, 1956

undertaking to keep faith. The pact thus made, with an elaborate form of words and gestures and a shared potion of which the oath-taker's blood made part, might be broken only at mortal peril and was therefore extremely binding. But was Mary not lending herself to "heathen devilry" and savage mumbo jumbo? Given the righteous mentality of the period, there must certainly have been those who thought so.

A glance at some of the actual cases takes us straight into the life of Ibibioland.

27th June, 1908

Ndta Ikot Obon v Asibon Ekanem

Charge Assault — stripping off Plaintiff's wife's cloth and insulting her naked in the market.

Defendant Not guilty. I went to buy produce, and she refused to sell, then when other sellers came the place was too straight [sic] for us and I made room with the good will of others. Then when we had words about the nuts not being full in the measure, she held me by my cloth. I told her to loose her hold on my cloth and she again took hold. That's why I took hold of her and her cloth was not well tied and it came off in my hand.

Adiaha Inyan wife in question sworn states. I refused to sell as I had bought for a customer, then when the person who had bought my nuts came, he wanted to throw my box and baskets aside, and I would not and he said Let me die when I reach Ibibio. I answered Let you die on the water going home. If I die, let you die too, I did you no harm, then he twice said curse words to me, and I laid hold of him and he took hold of my cloth and took it off and left me naked in the market place. The big man in the market asked him to make begging to me and make peace as this was bad, and he said Let her call me to Judgment, a woman from Ibibio, who is she to call me, [an] Ikpe.

Wife's statement corroborated by witnesses.

Judgment for Plaintiff. Defendant fined £3 or three months' H.L. [hard labour].

This had obviously been a magnificent market hullabaloo. The market superintendent had intervened to no effect. Female dignity is upheld.

Another case shows the new customs in conflict with the old. An outraged "husband" is trying to recover presents he had given a lady who lived with him for ten years, during which time he was trying to make up his mind to marry her in church.

9th July, 1909

Okpo Okok v Ekandem Nwa Etim

Claim to recover his marriage dowry, presents value £7 7s. 6d.

Plaintiff sworn states. I gave her gifts and I told her to lay them aside till I was ready to come with her into the Church. I was surprised then to find that she had put her name in the members class of the Church and I was angry. Then I got her own people to beg her as I was vexed at having been hasty. She would not listen when I offered twenty shillings as the Judges had ordered and she would not listen to my pleading. Then I got a small book [i.e. note] from Miss Slessor and I asked her to come there and judge between us. She would not come and so I took this action.

Defendant I have been with him as his friend wife since Coco Bassey died, he asked me from my mother and he gave me cloth and presents but he never asked me to lay them aside. He never sent me for an errand that I have refused. I have tried to be a good wife to him and I have not been idle. When he went to Calabar about five months ago, I put my name in the Church Candidates' class as I saw that I was a sinner, and when he came home he was angry. I told him that my only reason was that I wished to be good and do God's will. When I saw his anger I sent a person to plead with him to forgive me, and that is the only thing I know. He stopped me after I had cooked and counted his rods for a journey and said Woman, I tell you go from my house, you are not my wife any longer. I did not speak. He again ordered me to go and I did not speak. Then he lifted up his hand and swore by the God of Heaven, I order you to go out of this house. You are not my wife any longer. The man in whose shed we lived came then, but did not do anything and gave me shelter till the morning.

Mother of defendant corroborated defendant's witness.

A list of things given includes three times a bar of soap, a bottle of lemonade, two reels of cotton, one thimble 3d., fathoms of cloth, etc.

Judgment Court having asked whether you will pay her for ten years' service. You also put her out during the night. You refuse to marry her in the Christian fashion so that she could take you again as her husband. There is no claim on her for all her presents, she has worked for you.

Evidently the husband hoped to settle out of court with Mary's help, but the wife refused. It seems likely that she had got tired of waiting and had refused to live with him any longer unless he married her in church. It may be noted that he did not turn her out of the house until she had cooked his evening meal! Native law and custom seems to have been by-passed here in favour of women's rights and Christian matrimony. But in view of the presiding magistrate's well-known opinions it is difficult to see why the man brought an action.

Mary did not always act solely on the evidence before her. She often knew more about the case than came out in court and had no compunction about using this knowledge.

This is shown in a case in August 1909, where a woman was charged with putting white ants into a box in which important letters were kept. In her judgment Mary says: "Defendant has been troubling her house for years, first for divorce, then for everything." Clearly she knows the family history. In another case where plaintiff is trying to get a barrel of oil allegedly owed to him, Mary notes: "This palaver was on in Calabar in 1878!" She dismissed the case in 1905. One wonders if it is still going on.

Another case which may never have been settled was brought in August 1908. A woman sued her husband to recover her son. The details given are not very clear, and were apparently unsatisfactory. Mary notes that the defendant and plaintiff "spoke for an hour with no point". The court sent them off "till they got someone who knew what they wanted!"

Cases of unhappy marriages are common. A wife charges her husband with trying to poison her. He says, "Guilty. She has been a very bad wife to me. She also made me shame with walking naked on the street. I believe that the illness I am suffering from is her doing, so I said if I die she shall die also, and I did ask one man to kill her."

He is sent to prison for six months, the wife is given to her father, and the marriage is to be dissolved by the town when the husband is released. The wife leaves without repayment of dowry, however.

A wife sues her husband for support, saying he has left her alone for over two years. He pleads that he has not left her, but has been sick all the time. Mary notes, unsympathetically, "a big fat man", clearly not convinced about the sickness.

A man brings a case against his son-in-law, charging "killing his wife by sorcery and by medicine". The defendant appears to have behaved violently when his wife died in childbirth, and was reported to Miss Slessor. Mary's judgment is interesting. Both parties are to "chop mbiam" and the defendant, who must have been a Christian, is to swear on the Bible that he is innocent of the charge of "killing this woman and her child".

A little light relief is provided by a woman who sues to recover her "Auntly" title. The plaintiff says the defendant took his aunt and refuses to give her up. Defendant says he never heard of the woman. "Obviously lying", notes Mary. She ordered the defendant "to produce the woman and finish palaver". One would like to know more about this. Perhaps Auntie was useful in the market or as a baby-minder!

Twin murder does not figure in the list of charges since this would be a matter for a higher court, but Mary was actively engaged in trying to better the lot of the twin-mothers. In 1906 she wrote to Charles Partridge, "The twin-mothers from several districts have come at various times to me in order to get their lot made easier. I *forced* a number to come to court, but they were in terror for the chiefs taking revenge. The Enyon and Itu men spoke to the Ibibios, and comforted the women greatly, and sent proclamations to all parts, that each man was to care for his wife, and get a separate house built for them. Also the markets which prohibit them from buying and selling were warned to change their laws."

In November 1908, however, she must have succeeded in getting a test case brought to her court. A twin-mother brought a charge against a town for refusing to let her pass through. One man appeared as defendant.

Plaintiff I am a twin-mother. I am spokesman for the twin-mothers. This is the fourth time the whole town has come after me calling and hustling, but defendant was the only one who cursed me and said I had been bringing Ekpo to their town with my twin-mother's filthy accursed feet.

Defendant said they came through the town in the evening — they came inside my house.

Plaintiff said she went into a house on invitation but did not know defendant, swore on oath no twin-mother went through his yard.

Judgment for Plaintiff. The chiefs should have been here today. You are but a small boy [i.e. unimportant person]. The chiefs are at fault so the Court has pity on you. You can choose ten stripes or pay ten shillings and pay costs and from this day ANY woman shall walk on any road except a private house she shall not enter.

The chiefs had prudently stayed away, doubtless paying defendant to act as (quite literally) whipping boy. It is not recorded whether he chose the flogging or fine. The twin-mother would hardly have dared to bring such an action against a whole town if she had not been just a "spokesman" and perfectly confident of the outcome.

That this is the continuation of a long struggle (not completely won even today) is shown by the notice taken in the government's Annual Report for the previous year. It tells of the District Commissioner's success in getting husbands of twin-bearing women to take back their wives, by his summonsing the husbands for desertion and non-support, adding: "The result is a sign of the civilising influence worked through the Court by that admirable lady, Miss Slessor."

The Ikot Obong court records for the years during which Mary was magistrate do not reveal the strain of sitting for long hours in the broiling heat, sustained only by a tin of toffees, trying to shift a few grains of fact from floods of eloquence, exploding into violent indignation at times and boxing the ears of witnesses fool-hardy enough to tell lies. Nor the times when, having found against the litigants and fined them, she herself found work for them in the mission compound that would enable them to pay. Nor did she record, except occasionally in letters, the pressures exerted on her by relatives and friends of those concerned in the case.

Writing to Charles Partridge in February 1906, she described the trial of one Udo Antia, evidently a bad sort, although a chief and court member, and already under a two-year sentence from the district court:

Meanwhile his mother came in and she, expecting they would shoot him, hung on to me, lay on me, and hugged me for four long hours! I could not get out of her embraces until I was nearly fainting. "Take me, take him. Take me, take him. We will be your slaves for ever. Why did he not listen to you long ago when you called him? Etc., etc. He is all I have, *all*, all I have!" Until the chiefs were shedding tears. It was a bad hour for me, I tell you, for even Udo Antia is loved by a mother. What a mighty, what a mysterious thing is mother love! She coveted the chance of dying for him, and she crouched where her eyes devoured him, all the time of the trial, till she was so overcome they had to remove her.

He is eventually sentenced to a further two years imprisonment, whereon the magistrate steps out of her judicial role to comfort the old lady.

I told the mother I should look after her and her affairs, as her son had asked me, and begged her to let him go quietly.

Udo Antia's affairs crop up again in a letter to Charles Partridge in April. She says that all Udo's wives have gone off, now he is in prison, and she proposes to ask the District Commissioner "if these women may make 'friend' marriages [live 'in sin', no less] till he, Udo, comes home, and then go back to him with his children, as women here can't live single for years." To get the full impact of this remarkable suggestion one must remember that it is made by a middle-aged Scottish spinster working as a Presbyterian missionary in 1906! Whether the Mission Board would have appreciated this matter-of-fact recommendation may be doubted. It was almost certainly not consulted.

In February 1909, her health very poor, Mary considered giving up the court work. But the new District Officer asked her "so nicely" to stay on that she agreed to do so, holding court one day instead of two. But in November it came abruptly to an end. The circumstances which led to her resignation are not very clear and were never public, but can be partially reconstructed from her letters to Charles Partridge.

The administrative position in the District was evidently very shaky at this time, no one officer remaining in charge for more than a short time. One District Commissioner had died, another had blackwater fever and Mary believed it was a third who was carried past the church on a stretcher when she was conducting a service. With affairs in this state, a case was reported to Mary for investigation of a woman who had fallen in the bush, cut an artery and bled to death. Mary proceeded to act as coroner and gave the court messenger appropriate instructions, when another messenger from the Roads Department arrived to say it was a case of murder, which of course put it outside her normal jurisdiction. Mary, however, believing there was no-one on the government station in authority, simply sent a message back saying she had done all that was necessary and received from the new District Commissioner what she described as a "rhodomontade". She was so incensed by this—the man did not, of course, know her, but by this time she was accustomed to being known—that she wrote saying that she had "never interfered with a case being handled by the D.C.", could no longer serve under him, and sent in her resignation.

Her sense of injustice when that resignation was accepted ("I'm dismissed and that by utter strangers . . .") is not surprising—she had been in Calabar thirty-three years, since before many of the administrators were born. But her indignation over the whole episode suggests she set greater store by her court work than the Mission perhaps liked to think, enjoying its range and scope in spite of the heavy load it imposed.

Towards the end of her life, when she was tired and ill, people still looked to her for advice and help. Nor were all her fires damped down. Our old friend Udo Antia, now out of prison "by some wangle", continued to give trouble to the end. In 1914 Mary wrote resignedly, "Perhaps one of God's reasons for keeping me here so long is the keeping of such . . . characters in subjection and silence to a certain extent."

Mr. Maxwell said of Mary's early service as magistrate that the litigants emphatically got justice—sometimes more than they wished! From a strictly legal standpoint some of her judgments might be questioned. But they were accepted by a litigious and, indeed, quarrelsome people because she *knew* them, knew their language, understood and respected their customs. For in spite of the depths of human depravity into which her court work led her— "What a crowd of people I have had today and how debased!"—it was a labour of love. They knew this, accepted her justice, and never appealed against her judgments.

Like Christianity, the British system of justice gave most to those who previously had least—women and slaves. If not in strictest fact, then at least in spirit, Mary Slessor's was the court where no woman lost a case.

15

WITH SHOES OF PEACE

By FEBRUARY 1907 Mary's strength had given out. "I cannot walk now, nor dare I do anything to trifle with my health which is very queer now and then," she wrote, concluding that she would have to get a box on wheels made so that the children could *pull* her about. At last, however, she agreed to take her home leave.

In the nine years since she had last gone home, she had become a dominant figure in the Cross River region. Officials who availed themselves of her shrewd insight and experience were delighted to find her highly entertaining company—in some moods an inveterate comic. When she was finally persuaded to travel, they passed her tenderly from hand to hand all the way home, much concerned for her wellbeing.

This time Jean stayed behind to keep house for the younger children and an eye on things in general. She could stand in for "Ma" in school and church and was thought to be a "lovely reader". It was the earnest seven-year-old Dan who now ran Mary's errands, pushed her bike up hills, served her at meals and escorted her to Scotland.

As before, she went straight to the home of the devoted M'Crindles. They were shocked at the way the last years had aged her. She was frail and shrunken and looked, as she described herself, an old lady. Her sprightly letters had made it hard to envisage anyone so physically exhausted. Yet she gathered strength quickly and was soon visiting friends in other towns. John M'Crindle wrote:

> One afternoon she arrived home to us after visiting some friends in Dundee. She was somewhat worn out, as she had had a slight attack of fever to which she was constantly subject, and sitting down at the tea table, all alone, she lifted her head and uttered these words, "Thank ye, Faither, ye ken I'm tired," as if she had been speaking to one of us.

A few elderly Church people still remember the worn, austere woman with the unexpectedly sweet voice, dry wit and mis-

chievous laugh—and round-eyed Dan in all the glory of knicker-
bocker suits. Gifts and mechanical toys—a watch and clockwork
train—were heaped on the delighted child until Mary feared he
would be spoilt.

The little boy soaked up experiences to last him the rest of his
life. He gorged on fresh plums at tea with Mina Amess and her
family at Stanley. He fought pillow fights, with the Daniel Mac-
Arthur whose namesake he was, in a shared bedroom in the manse
at Bowden, next door to Mary's friend, Miss Adam. He was as fas-
cinated by white children as they were by him, for in those days
European homes on the west coast of Africa were uniformly child-
less. Such white women as came out at all went home early in
pregnancy and returned to Africa, if they did so, leaving their babies
behind. Mary herself considered it a "sin against the child" when
Dr. Robertson and his wife brought their small daughter to Itu.

Daniel MacArthur, now living in Oban, remembers Mary as a
formidable figure whose word was law and whose breakfast tray he
carried up with trepidation. It is clear that Mary's willingness to
defy the Foreign Mission Committee was the talk of the good
minister's household. Revered figure that she now was, no one
would gainsay her. He recalls how, as the whole family were hurrying to a meeting where several hundred people had gathered to hear
Mary speak, she marched the two boys, on impulse, into a photographer's to have their picture taken, a thing not done in a moment.
Yet this was surely no idle whim but a move to establish that the
"black and white Dans"—as they were called—were not creatures
apart but could stand up and be seen to be friends, a thing they have
remained to this day.

Mary rode out with the well-to-do Miss Adam in her carriage in
Bowden; cycled, much alarmed by the motor traffic, with Miss
Amess in Stanley; shopped, somewhat guiltily, for "frills and fur-
belows" in Edinburgh; and strolled the streets of Dundee by
Baxter's Mill and the Queen Street Mission with girlhood friends.
No doubt she also saw to those mundane repairs of teeth and
spectacles, shoes and luggage, that even she could not wholly avoid.

But she missed her real life, especially her "bairns". She felt
strange writing her letters without a toddler balanced on one foot or
nursling asleep in her lap under the writing-pad and would beg to be
allowed to hold the pink Scottish babies. Most of all, however, she
was anxious about her big girls, undefended in Ibibioland. In native
law a single woman was wholly unprotected. "If she be not man's
wife", Mary wrote, "she may be insulted or injured with impunity,

no punishment except the merest rebuke can be meted to the man." It was to be feared the local Lotharios would consider Jean and the others fair game. Unpleasant (though unspecified) rumours had already reached her. Long before her friends considered her fit to return, or Dan felt ready to relinquish his delicious notoriety, she booked her return passage to Calabar.

Two projects were uppermost in her mind as she returned. One was the establishment of her long-projected Industrial Training Centre for women. The other was to make good her promise to the young men of Ikpe Ikot Nkun, who had sought her help several years before.

Good news awaited her in that a Miss Peacock and a Miss Reid were shortly to take over the station at Ikot Obong (apart from the court work) and leave her free to carry out her plan for Use. Having assured herself that the rumours about her girls were no more than malicious gossip, she set her family to work preparing both houses for occupation.

At last, only two miles away, she had companions eager to help her. Mary tells how they came to start up work in an abandoned road camp.

Last week . . . the two ladies at Ikot Obon who are very enthusiastic and keen, thought we might all take a turn round that side of the country and see if we could send out some farther help into the darkness. We ran on and on till we reached that old camp, and found that the tornado and wet seasons had made a wreck of the roof, and that passers-by had taken the woodwork for fire-wood, and the grass and bush was up to the very doors. Still the site is good and high, and lovely water runs quite close, with sandy bed. So there and then the impulse came to take and work it up into an out station, or at least a Resting House from which we could reach several villages round about, sleeping there for a night or two and cooking there. After two days' thought, I told the ladies, and it seemed to them just what we should do. So we all went down to the Engineer in charge of the Rds. Dept. and asked if we might have the place, and if so cd he hire men for us who could put the roof right, and make bamboo slides for doors, and kindle fires to dry out the softened mud floors and to cut the bush down, and he was more than kind and said he would see to the whole thing. And so yesterday morning early he sent a dozen men with a very good Xtian boy for head man, and I told them all we wanted, and gave them some money to give the chiefs of the town, in order to get bamboos and mats from their land. This morning a man came with a coconut husk stuck full of sharpened spikes, which was put at the back of the camp to poison their feet, and he said the chiefs were sulky, and said they did not want money and would not let anyone go for mats, and all the head boy could beg or say, they would not "open their faces" to him, as we say here.

I am very sorry, as it is the first rebuff I have ever had, and I can't think what the reason is. I know it has not anything to do with the Gospel! The villages lie far off the road so when we were there we did not see any of the people of that town, as a rainstorm came on and drove us home. So I just sent word to the lads to go and tell them it was our gospel work and school we wished to start, and please not to let any other thing that vexed them stand in God's way, as we meant to help them . . . I shall see the chiefs myself on Friday I hope and put the matter right. I have no doubt it will be put straight when we are face to face, and then I hope your money will be the beginning of a new work in a quiet way. We can do it between us three, till we get the confidence of the people and the affection of the bairns and then perhaps we can get a couple of school lads to go, and come home for the week ends, working on till they shall have the sabbath also for the miles round them, in which is still the seat of Satan.

The planting of the spikes proved, as Mary expected, to be due to a misunderstanding, which was soon cleared up.

Mary's plan for the Women's Settlement was to bring out, with the help of a private donation, a worker who could train women in a few basic skills that would render them independent. Basket-making for the government building projects (where every ounce of sand or cement had to be transported on the labourers' heads) was to be the first project.

The settlement should be self-sufficient. There was ample space at Use for raising food and keeping livestock, and surplus produce could be marketed at Okopedi beach, only two miles away. Mary planted fruit seedlings and considered raising rubber and cocoa as commercial products. Only details remained to be agreed with the Mission Council.

But the "details" proved to include a stipulation that Mary should stay at Use for at least a year to put the settlement on an organised footing. At this, Mary took instant fright. Her talents did not lie in institutional work and she refused to be tied down. She declared

that the money given her might just as well be used for expansion
with the result that—though the few women already settled on the
place appear to have stayed on, farming in a small way—the project
petered out. Doubtless there were some wry faces in mission circles
when its instigator resumed her free-lancing existence.

Her element was the wild places, and even these quickly grew too
tame. In the next few years she was rarely well and never still. On
foot, bike or canoe she travelled, fanning any spark of interest among
the people. She was the feet of the Church and those feet could not
rest.

She did not despise comfort. She would revel in the unexpected
gift of a mattress or carpet or the sweets of which she was so fond.
But she wanted nothing, would spend nothing on, herself. Like the
Africans, she was adept at contrivance. When a visitor to Use wanted
to make an early-morning start, Mary simply grabbed a cock that
was running loose in the compound, tied it to the sheet of corrugated
iron overlaid with a mattress that was her bed, and no alarm clock
was needed.

Nor were her movements random. Though she cast about in
many directions, she took no definite step without a sure sense of
God's purpose for her. Only then would she move. Ikpe, a busy
market from which a whole new population could be reached,
seemed to her as strategically attractive as Itu had been. But, much
as she wanted to go there, it was a trying, time-consuming journey
from Use, and the year 1909 put so many obstacles in the way of her
going that she began to doubt if this was what the Lord wanted her
to do.

First there was her own wretched health. She had a period of
excruciating suffering with boils all over her head and face. Then
Jean was ill in hospital in Calabar for several months (probably with
a female complaint, for the next year Mary wrote, "The Doctor says
Jean must not marry.")

There was an official Mission visit—deputies from Scotland to
be shown around—and a Royal Commission investigating the rights
and wrongs of the liquor trade, before which Mary, one of its fierce
critics, was summoned to appear. Her court work, soon to come to
an ignominious end, was particularly heavy in the absence of any
consecutive authority at the District Office, where illness and death
had decimated the staff.

In October sixteen-year-old Mary was married from the Use
house, in the little mud church. Annie, the good-hearted field
worker, had already married a trader active in the church, Akpan

Inyang. But Mary, the "child of wonder", was a particular favourite, and her betrothed something of a local celebrity; he was the driver of that new-fangled wonder, the government Ford truck, David Adeyemo. Mary wrote fondly:

> . . . yesterday our Mary was married to a young Lagos man who is in the engineering and motor department of government work. He is Xtian and is well educated . . .

Dan and Asuquo had by now been packed off to the Hope Waddell Institute for their education, so that the family had shrunk to four. But the newly-weds lived near and were frequent visitors, the bride often arriving "full of importance" in the car, usually with gifts for the family. And that Christmas, when Mary was again nearly blind with a fresh crop of boils, they received many kind attentions. The Governor sent up a case of milk and Charles Partridge, now i Lagos, decided Mary must have worn out her old bicycle and sent her a new one.

It was to their new "brother-in-law" that the children appealed when Mary fell desperately sick with dysentery in the spring. He informed the District Commissioner who immediately dispatched the car to take her into hospital at Itu.

There was consternation among the white community at her breakdown. No one had really thought it could happen. She was considered indestructible. While she slowly convalesced at the home of the young Macgregors in Calabar, a concerted effort was made to equip her house at Use with a rainwater catchment and to install (and try to persuade Mary to *use*) a water filter.

Mary, however, did not look on these weeks of invalidism as a warning but rather threw herself, the moment she could summon an ounce of strength, into the frenzy of activity of one who knows there is little time to lose. Work was her cure. "I begin every day, almost every journey in pain, and in such tiredness that I am sure I can't go on, and whenever I begin, the strength comes, and it increases."

She visited Ikpe, which was not distant as the crow flies but involved a two-stage journey, by canoe to Arochuku, then on foot and again by canoe to Ikpe. It was a gruelling journey for a sick woman, but was repeated several times in the latter half of 1910, once in the company of the Macgregors. When they joined her at Use she was prostrate with fever and they assumed the trip would be cancelled. But at one o'clock in the morning they heard her up and about, organising the packing for a moonlight start at three.

They appealed to Jean to stop her but Jean shrugged and said, "She is often like that, and gets better on the road."

Mary's expedient for travelling when in such a state of health was to take as big a dose of laudanum as she dared, wrap up in a blanket and lie in the bottom of the canoe. Thus, she declared, she "managed fine".

And in her company most journeys had amusing moments. She and Miss Peacock once landed together at a beach where the women were totally naked but for their colourful head-ties. Mary, reminded of Biblical strictures in the matter of headcovering, shot a wry glance at her companion and murmured, "D'ye doubt the Apostle Paul was here before us!"

To a band of girls who supported her work she began a merry account of one of her journeys with, "I wish the mosquitoes were just half as tired as I am, I would then perhaps write better . . .

I shall be glad to be in the canoe and rest. I do not believe all the long two days' journey will tempt me even to read a paper. I shall just lie and revel in the rest. Only mind, it is a cram! It would be a rare treat to you young folk, with your ignorance of back-ache, and with your supple limbs; indeed, I believe it would be a jolly trip for you. There will be Jean, Alice, Maggie, Whitie and two infants, with their paraphernalia of milk and water &c., &c., all crushed up into a space of four feet by two, and flies will be biting, and girls will be screaming, and the canoe boys will be sometimes singing and sometimes quarrelling, and sometimes splashing us and one another with water from the paddles. Then there will be an alligator to shout at and throw things at, if it is at a safe distance. If not, to dodge him will give mirth. Then it will be a wildfowl, then a monkey, then a snake paddling across, and then a bump on a sunken tree, and we will all be thrown anyhow, and some of the boys, if punting, will be sure to go overboard, and then the screaming!

One would not guess from this how perilous it still could be to go adventuring in the country between the Cross River and the Niger. Though white people were generally well received—and Mary rightly deemed that a woman accompanied only by children disarmed fear—there were isolated pockets of country where an outsider stirred deep-ingrained suspicion and might be slaughtered on sight. In 1905 a medical officer, having lost his way and wandered into a strange village, was killed and eaten. The next year an Assistant District Commissioner was murdered. Daniel Slessor says that the roads west of Ikot Ekpene were considered dangerous because of "headhunters" as late as 1920. Though these fears were probably exaggerated, there must have been considerable apprehension felt each time Mary branched out afresh, and the children who went with her needed courage.

Mary began building at Ikpe in 1910 in spite of her profound weariness and the admittedly swampy nature of the land awarded her by the chiefs. Until a hut was built she lived in the unfinished church. "I am committed now ... No more idleness for me. I am entering in the dark as to how and where and when. How I am to manage I do not know, but my mind is at perfect peace about it, and I am not afraid. God will carry it through. The Pillar leads." For, she wrote in another place, "It is not a question how much we can do with our own hands, or our own minds, or our own lives. It is always a question how much we are willing to let God do with them."

Once more she was in the thick of life, directing labour, nursing abandoned babies and quieting the people's fears. As of old, she intervened to quell a market riot that was being fought with sticks and matchets by seizing the wrists of the antagonists and insisting the matter be settled by "palaver". When government sanitary inspectors escorted by police came to vaccinate the villagers and were promptly driven off, she sent for the lymph herself and cajoled the people into submitting to immunisation.

> The people here [she wrote] are willing to be vaccinated if Ma or a white man will do it, but they will not have it from these black boys, as they are full of *mischief*, i.e. sorcery or witch. The black man has no faith in his fellow black man.

Ikpe was obviously a job for someone younger and Mary dared hope that, once the work was begun, two women might be appointed to carry it on. She even proposed sacrificing her own salary "if the wherewithal should fail ... I shall only be too glad to live on native food with my bairns."

But there were misgivings about the suitability of Ikpe as a station. Young Dr. Hitchcock, sent up to investigate, confirmed that its situation was anything but healthy. No one was surprised, however, to learn that his findings had not altered Miss Slessor's determination to work there. She said to Dan, "God sent me here, and I am prepared to die here."

No one else, however, could be expected. So, for the next three years, she had no choice but to alternate between Ikpe and Use, always sick at heart because going to one meant leaving the other "shepherdless".

But it was an exhilarating time nonetheless — what she termed "a real life . . . not all preaching and holding meetings, but rather a life and an atmosphere which the people can touch and live in and be made willing to believe in when the higher truths are brought before them. In many ways it is a prosaic life, dirt and dust and noise and silliness and sin in every form, but full, too, of the kindliness and homeliness and dependence of children who are not averse to be disciplined and taught, and who understand and love just as we do. The excitements and surprises and novel situations would not, however, need to be continuous, as they wear and fray the body, and fret the spirit and rob one of sleep and restfulness of soul."

16

DEAR MR. PARTRIDGE

FROM THE TIME when Mary crossed the river to Itu, in 1904, to the end of her life, she was associated with many young administrative officers, making common cause with them over matters like sanitation, vaccination, education and the leasing of land. Drawn together in the lonely forefront of advancing civilisation, they offered one another hospitality, shared transport and pooled information.

The men came and went with dizzying frequency, on annual leave, sick leave, transfer or, too often — dressed in formal suits they had not failed to have by them for the occasion — into graves in some forest clearing. They might sometimes be ignorant, arrogant or obtuse, but at their best they tackled their problems with energy and commonsense and without the severe moral opprobrium that irritated Mary in her fellow missionaries.

Many of them took a sceptical view of missionary endeavour. Their own approach to the people was more that of a school prefect who recalls what it was like to be a turbulent, lower-school ignoramus and is determined to see fair play. They were "gentlemen" in the specific Victorian sense and sometimes seemed to Mary too "fine" for the tasks that awaited them. But they were all "somebody's bairns" and she felt privileged by age and experience to love, tease and admonish them as she saw fit. Even a Provincial Commissioner was not surprised to be sent off with the words, "And see ye be a guid laddie!"

They, in turn, expanded in the warmth of Mary's interest in them, appreciating her original turn of mind and impudent disdain of authority. She corresponded with many of them long after they had left the coast.

Charles Partridge, the first District Commissioner with whom she worked in active partnership, kept the letters she wrote him. Years after her death he presented them, along with some Efik books and the gramophone record he had made of her speaking the parable of the Prodigal Son, to the Dundee Museum.

There were men who played a more active part in her life. But the letters make it clear that Partridge set a standard for working officers with which few others could compete. Together they planned the future of the newly opened district of Ikot Ekpene in that first, excitingly mobile period after the destruction of the Long Juju. Their relationship was for both of them fruitful at the most thoughtful level of their lives — and was deepened and intensified by the lonely isolation in which they lived.

Their backgrounds were totally different. Partridge had been born at Offton Place, Suffolk, was a Cambridge graduate (1895) and M.A. (1901) and had lived some years in France. There was a wide disparity of ages. He was thirty-three, Mary fifty-six, when they met. Yet Mary's letters to him suggest a high degree of mutual understanding. More frankly personal than her letters to Church friends, which were often printed and passed round for general edification, they provide an illuminating glimpse into the last years of her life.

The woman Charles Partridge met can have had little surface appeal. Sickness and struggle had exhausted Mary's pleasant looks. Pictures show a gaunt, stiff-backed woman in whose face is written the grim struggle against bodily failing. Her clothes were a matter of indifference to her and she did not always remember to wear her teeth. He may have been greatly surprised by the warm, almost girlish, spontaneity of the first notes she wrote him. But he knew her value from the start. It began with the gift of a Christmas pudding.

> Dear Mr. Partridge,
> I can't help it! I must write a "Thank you" for such a lovely huge pudding! I'm only afraid I shan't get a chance to send part of it to the dear sister at Okoyong [Miss Wright] and the bairns. We had nothing at all to differentiate last Xmas from the other days . . . and this will be such a treat. It is simply lovely! Surely it is a home-made one? And what about the basin? Am I to keep that too? . . .

The District Commissioner, well aware of what he would owe to Miss Slessor's good offices in a district where customary rites were said to include cannibalism, human sacrifice and twin murder, had respectfully sought guidance. Her reply should be emblazoned on the heart of every man or woman who has to do with an alien people:

> See how much more likely they are to fear you than to give themselves over at once . . . If you can discriminate between fear and stubbornness, you have won half the battle.

Twelve days later, with the friendly preamble, "Here I am already meddling in your affairs", she sent him a "palaver" between Ibibio and Calabar with explicit advice on how to settle it:

> *If it commends itself to you*, could you not meet with Mr. Maxwell [District Commissioner in Calabar] in order to gain the confidence and obedience of these people to make them our allies instead of our enemies ... *Give the two sections strong Mbiam*, that if the one side went with deceit and told lies on the other to the white man, or to the Calabar judge, let *Mbiam* treat with them, etc., etc. .... Be as just as you like, and as severe, only *show them the reason patiently*.

In April he was expected at Itu and she grieved that she could not offer him hospitality, ". . . but here are three infants and a small crowd in my one shanty, and they are usually most musical in the evening and we get dinner as best we can . . ."

A fortnight later she was in a flurry of delighted confusion at discovering him to be an author. His *Cross River Natives* had recently been published and he had sent her a copy.

> What a fraud you are! Here is you with a record of observation and research; and half the letters of the alphabet running after your name and you speaking as if you were the merest beginner . . . Fancy having a piece of work like this over and above doing a D.C.'s work and in a new district, too . . . The natives have seldom had an interpreter so absolutely truthful and free from prejudice. It is so seldom that one sees anything from this coast that is not embroidered. Your narrative from beginning to end is faithful to the life, minus the imagination which even the D.C.s love to weave around their yarns and tell on the spot. I wish you had let yourself go a little, though, in regard to nature . . .
>
> It is such a pleasure to meet a man who cares for more than the small talk and the inanities of conventional life out here . . .

On the 18th June she wrote:

> It seems like years since I saw you. You have had more bother, I hear, and will be tired-er still. Well, well, it's all in a day's work, I suppose, and calmer days will soon come . . .

At his urging, she has been prospecting for sites and has chosen Ikot Obong.

> I would . . . try to make this the first of a chain of stations, going farther in with rest-houses like yours, where a native boy

could stay and carry on small elementary schools . . . I had a letter from the H.C.'s office, asking if I should take the Vice-Presidentship [of the native court] and I answered in the affirmative . . .

By October she was sufficiently settled in Ikot Obong to take up her court duties.

30th October, 1905

Dear Mr. Partridge,

Your messenger has brought up mails for me and at the same moment they have brought two men implicated in the death of a man here. He has taken poison bean and then hung himself . . .

Thanks ever so much for the carpenter. He has hung two doors for me today, so I feel at home and private now.

Your boy wants to push on and my head is reeling with this gory story.

Kindest regards and thanks for books and papers . . .

In December his tour was already over. Again he sent her his pudding. On Christmas Day she sent him an almanac with good wishes for his coming leave and thanks for "the cheerful helpful friendship which has gladdened the last year's journey".

Poor health kept him home for over a year while Mary kept him up to date with local news. She sought advice as to where she should go if she got the chance to move on, and declared firmly that whatever the Presbytery said about returning to Okoyong, she would "simply refuse to go". Of Calabar's changing scene she wrote:

Gaiety will be the order of the day now. All the Europeans are to have their wives now, which will be a good thing for them and for the country. There's your chance. I'll be an aunty to you both . . .

Charles kept her supplied with books from home, which she criticised with shrewd insight. He also scolded her (a recurrent theme) for neglecting her health.

30th April

Your long breezy letter came last night—shall I confess it?—when I was struggling vainly to throw off a bit of fever. But I *had* been taking quinine, and as Miss Amess is with me, I *have* been using filtered water, so you can't crow over a victory . . .

She was lukewarm in her approval of his "good and conscientious" successor at Ikot Ekpene:

... I prefer Mr. Partridge's methods. Detail and red Tape is most obnoxious here at the moment. Still, it is a great blessing to have a gentleman to work for and with.

Partridge had evidently discouraged Mary's hopes that he might return with a wife (he was, in fact, to remain a bachelor) and, furthermore, expressed disapproval of men who did so. Mary retorted with vehemence:

I need not say I do not share your opinion about men marrying who are engaged here. Women are as eager to share in all the work and sacrifice of the world as men, and it is their privilege to share it, and it is their mission to be the motive power, and the steadying and inspiring power in a man's life, and so you are keeping some good woman out of her place of privilege and work and are depriving yourself of God's greatest gift outside of the spiritual world, in refusing to accept it.

The only surprise he had for her when he returned in November was the phonograph which so captured her imagination. Mary was greatly gratified by his approval of all that had been accomplished at Ikot Obong in his absence. But his was a busy life ("There is such a constant strain on a D.C. I should be a street-sweeper sooner, I think . . .") and she seems to have found it no easy matter to capture his attention long enough to make arrangements for handing over her official work when she herself was preparing to go home.

Use. 2 April, 1907

O Mr. Partridge!!!! I simply don't know what to say!! and I have been fairly crying because you went past and didn't call . . . Mr. Russell [a local trader] was *quite sure* you would not stop at Ikotobon. Now you are, and if this lovely cloak would let me, I would sleep. I'm so glad I can talk to you.

I've waited in the house for five days in order to talk to you about the Court, if I go home, and Mr. Gray came up this afternoon and settled everything about my going with Mr. Middleton of Lagos who has offered to take me to Edinburgh, and he leaves in May. And now comes this cloak, which says, "Here your needs are all met." It is simply wonderful, except for you! I'm sure I ought to go, but if it all adds to your burden, I would rather stay . . .

She went, however, and from Forcados, on the 20th May, sent him congratulations on his appointment to Calabar. She was grieved, however, for the Ikot Ekpene chiefs, "who will be afraid of a new man". Her next was from Scotland.

> My dear kind patient old chief,
> ... Winter could not be much worse, and where are the roses and the strawberries and the beauty of the traditional June? I am not feeling patriotic at all ... I am very, very well all the same, and as fat and as hungry as ever I was in my young days. I shall be out again in no time if this goes on. I can walk ... I am only afraid of the traffic and these awful motor cars ...

In July she thanked him for ordering male visitors off from the Use house. "The girls say no one bothers them and for that I have to thank you". In September,

> ... I have been visiting old friends and am just overwhelmed with the love and kindness of all. It is just restful to be called by your Christian name and to hear people say, "How like your mother you are ..."

She was, she said, "revelling in frocks and furbelows"

> ... But all this is most unbecoming in the senior member of a Presbyterian Mission! So you must keep my weakness a secret. I am trying to take the plainest and cheapest of frocks out with me. Only fancy them telling me that my costume is like a bride's rig-out! Really, the three junior Mission ladies, Misses Peacock, Reid and Amess, told me that when we all met the other day in Glasgow, and I confess to feeling ashamed to be in grey silk, when they were so modestly and consistently garbed in navy blue, and I could be the mother of the lot! Oh, well, it's my last shew-off, so I may be pardoned. Anaemic and debilitated or not, I am *not* well pleased at their leaving the station, and I should like to see the man at Church Council who could *make* me leave any place ...

Continuing this letter ("Dear Old Ruler") on the 3rd October, she has heard that he is invalided home and is full of sympathy. She *should* (she says) tell him it serves him right for being such an agnostic, but declares instead, "You are just a dear good old man, and I *cannot believe* that you will not go back to your work ... Have you good reading? It is such a help to keep off nervousness and weariness to have a good book."

She herself has had "a severe month of it" but is now "cycling all over the country and behaving like a young lady". She has been urged to stay on in Scotland to gain strength and undertake a speaking tour, and comments tartly, "As if I could, at my age, do one and gain the other!" Anyway, "I can't see my way to wait, because of the empty station and my big girls."

From aboard the *Fantee*, on October 25th, she complained of the "tameness and exactions" of life at home.

> Life is so full of conventional duties, which are as hard in their way as the real things of life, but much less satisfactory. Still, I have enjoyed it, the whitewashings and pullings about to get me into society shape notwithstanding. I hope I shall be more civilised and Christian in my way of life for it all . . .

Her prescription for Charles's recovery was work and (she begs him not to be angry) trusting in the Lord to heal — "A way which I have proved often." As to the work,

> Write! It will only need a beginning. What has been done. What may be done. What should have been done in the Protectorate. The native, his habits, life and laws, etc., the country, its produce, its possibilities, etc. but please leave *religion* out this time, as I don't deem you fit to write on such a wide and inward subject. I think one should be surer and more strictly *located*, if I may say so. Your ideas on that subject are too loose and disjointed, and take too little reck of such facts as SIN . . .

Charles, unfortunately, did not heed this advice. His next book was an unconvincing romance in the Rider Haggard vein, disappointing compared with his first. Nor did his religious views become "located" in Mary's sense. In an article contributed to the *East Anglian Daily Times* eighteen years later, he described himself as a "pagan overlaid with a very thin veneer of Christianity". But he retained a strong interest in the subject.

Mary returned to Ikot Obong. But the *rapport* that had existed between her and the administration while Partridge was District Commissioner was not to be recovered. Her letter of January 1908 had a faintly disconsolate tone.

> . . . A white man passed on Monday as I taught school at Use. I bowed. He lifted his hat and walked on. Mr. Rosario (of the Road Department) is my only friend here and the factory folk and they are most kind. Rosario could not be kinder if he was my brother. He brought up all my provisions, nineteen boxes, without my asking . . . He came up on Christmas Day, and sent me a ham and plum pudding, and here he is again lest I should be lonely. But

I'm wearying to see you again, for your place can't be filled by any of the others, good as they are.

She continued to entertain him in his convalescence in faraway Suffolk with comment on the books he has sent her. One can imagine his amusement on reading her assertion that the "old-world gentle-women" of one novel were more to her taste than the "new woman". "I'm too old for the new, clever, independent brand, I fear." She passed on the news and gossip of Ibibioland, too, and when he complained that she did not answer his questions precisely enough promised, in chastened tone, to try, relieved that he was well enough to be "cantankerous". On the subject of the romance he was writing, she issued a timely warning:

Do not let your imagination get the upper hand . . . It is one of God's greatest gifts to man, but unless it is in a world of facts and forces, and has to play the game of give and take to the full, it will lead you to be a dreamer of dreams and a seer of visions, and a D.C. — no pun meant — must be made of sterner stuff than mystics are fashioned from. So keep your inner optics in good order and training . . .

It was to his "dreams" that she attributed what she described as "the best joke of the season". For he had written flatteringly of her "very pretty hair", teasingly suggesting that she went hatless out of vanity.

A good many have shared the joke and it isn't finished yet. I was "Carrots" and "Fire" to my brothers and sisters, and my poor hair was the bane of my girlhood, so much did I dread the "Carrots" part of it, and now in my old age it has "gold glints" in the sun. Yes, *in the sun*!! The poor half-dozen white threads that barely covered the scalp during my last two or three years have multiplied exceedingly during my trip to Bonnie Scotland, but alas! that the "Carrots" should have developed into a baser metal than gold, with which even the sun cannot conjure!! So, dear boy, prepare for disillusionments, and if I take your advice — as I did last Sunday after reading your epistle — know for a truth that it is not for health reasons that I wear a hat, but because there is nothing left on my pate to glint! . . . Yes, I took your advice. I never once removed my hat all day, from 7 a.m. to 8 p.m. and before I was at Use, I had fever. It is the first time in my experience I have been able to keep my hat on so long, and the woeful result is quite the unexpected. I am sleeping sometimes, when it is not *too* hot—under a net. I *have* several times during this term taken quinine. I am drinking from a . . . sparklet—the filter I may indulge in soon, and I WORE MY HAT, will that satisfy you?

After a year at home, however, Partridge recovered and Mary urged him to bring back an heiress and a motor car. With his return imminent, she wrote, "Glorious news! . . . Come on, old man, with or without the heiress! It is all one so be you come." But on the 17th July: "What a sell! What a dead-down dump!" His posting was to Lagos, nearly four hundred miles away.

A month later she was regretting he could not see her rejuvenated by a new set of teeth—"when I don't forget to put them in, and with my 'pretty hair' as thick, tho' more silvern, than it ever was . . . I run on my bike like a youngster." Her powers of recuperation were not far short of miraculous, for renewed zest in life is evident in every line of a hilarious letter penned on the 15th September— Mary's answer to the many new developments Charles has described in his part of the country.

My dear old Boss,
 . . . Your description makes my teeth water . . . I'll be over by first excursion boat! Aro *Railway* Station!!! Our motor visits and our telegraph line are not much after that!!! Send round your Poulterer, please, and your Dairyman!!! I'm quite in an envious mood!! And really I must try to have an airplane or something constructed to link this benighted place with Neko. I've done my best here, for I've bought a cow. A man in trouble in Ikot Obon was to give it to Halliday [the Court Clerk] for fifty shillings which was shamefully low, and H. has no place for a cow, without being a nuisance to the gardens around, so I gave seventy shillings and the cow has been added to the menagerie. She took us all in tow the first week, every night and morning, and gave us a run through bush and everything till of course we had to let go, and then we had mild excursions all over the bush with an occasional race after her again, till again she took the rope, and thus we played in the moonlight, till I was at my wits' end, and everything was broken to pieces. My hands are wounded still. . . One night she took the young men of Use for a run and had them up well on the road to Ikot Obon, but at length she did arrive dragging four or five of them, and she was kept a prisoner with grass and water in her room. Speak of milking the creature! But she lets me scratch her nose now, and she came home with Jean tonight quite

quietly. So I shall try to tame and pet her, and perhaps in the future we, too, may have fresh milk, *not necessarily* out of whisky bottles.

This obstreperous animal became notorious in the district as "Ma Slessor's coo".

In 1909 Mary's health dwindled again ("I have just lain down every time I have had a spare bit of time, for the reason that my poor back will not 'sit up'.") and when she visited Calabar, in July, to testify before a Commission of Inquiry into the Liquor Trade, her run-down condition produced agonising symptoms.

Use Ikot Oku
7/7/09

Very dear old friend,

I only got your telegram last week. I went to the "Commissioner", and went very ill, with at least one hundred boils over my head. But that was not nearly enough. I lay down, or stretched across is nearer the thing, Mrs. Wilkie's bed and for a whole month was in one prolonged agony of pain. The boils came in shoals over my face, till you would not have recognised me . . . whenever I got rested from one operation of having the cores pressed out, another began, and I cried like a child when I was not shrieking, all the long weeks. No sleeping draught could keep out the pain. I am a very shaky bundle of nerves down to this hour. I could not see to read if I had been able, for my eye-lids were full . . . I have often written and joked with you about the "pretty hair" and the halo. Poor hair! Poor head! It is as bald as a six-pence now all over the back, and I wear a H.K.F. knotted at the four corners as we did in school days . . . the few hairs left on the front are like those of a doll's head put on with bad glue . . . The Dr. never saw anything like it . . .

Partridge, horrified by this account, seems to have said she should pack it in and go home instead of making a martyr of herself, for in October, after giving him a full account of Mary's wedding, she retorted with vehemence:

I love my Master, and I will not go out from Him, and I do believe that I am doing Ikpe and Use good by giving them that which takes away the hunger of the spirit, and gives them a definite *tangible* Helper and hope and life. So there!!! As long as I can nurse a motherless bairn, or help to keep peace in a home or town, or be a mother to my own bairns, I'm to stick to my post, and you would be the first to cry shame if I turned tail for a bit of fever, or even a bald head. My hair is growing nicely and I hope it will be quite covering the scalp before you come over to see me.

Partridge's return to Ikot Ekpene, often rumoured, never came to pass, but his attentions to Mary continued. To him, and probably to no one else, she confided the whole distressing story of her resignation from the court work, knowing he would understand both the confusion of the situation and the officiousness of certain administrators.

Most years he remembered to send her a Christmas pudding, a thoughtful and sentimental act recalling the start of their friendship. In 1910 he dispatched from Lagos a new bicycle to replace the hard-used old one.

"Oh, you dear!" she exclaimed, as excited as a child. But the writing of this letter is almost illegible. "I have still this gouty Calabar swelling and can't hold the pen, my thumb is so sore . . ."

A month later: ". . . I'm almost blind, I've had that head and neck of boils again." But Ikot Ekpene boasted a doctor whose treatment "killed the hundreds of things and made life bearable again".

In June, after the most protracted illness yet, she wrote from Duke Town, "O you dear duffer—will that do?" For he has demurred at the "Dear Mr. Partridge" of her previous (semi-official) letter and asked if they are no longer friends. She protests at length and with touching insistence.

Yet, as the years passed the exchange of letters became more sporadic. Mary, when she did not hear from him, feared she had somehow given offence and was more than a little offended herself. She worried for fear he was sick or had gone home or lest "something had turned you from me".

After the contretemps that led to her resigning her court work, successive District Commissioners had given her a wide berth, not always paying her even the courtesy of calling. She complained she did not receive so much as "the scratch of a pen". The management of her people's affairs, so natural to her, was in other hands. She felt cast aside, no longer trusted, a "social leper".

She herself must have become more difficult than the calm tenor of her letters suggests, fiercely resenting young men who did not share her way of thinking. She is glad not to have to travel in the same launch with one—"or there would have been a sparring match". Of another she sniffs, "The first gentleman we have had for years."

One incident she relates must have amused Partridge:

... This morning I have just answered a very prudish epistle from a black clerk asking me to tell my church member women to cover their nakedness when they pass here, "else I shall make the boys *drove* them away". Rather a tall order, seeing ... the ford where the women cross the creek to their farms ... takes them up to the armpits. *I've answered him.*

Though Partridge, immersed in the affairs of the Yorubas in the West, wrote less often and probably with less eagerness for the news of Ibibio, she continued to regale him with the details of any outstanding event. And, describing her own great public moment in 1913, when the Order of St. John of Jerusalem was bestowed upon her, she hastened to say that she felt the unworthiness of being so singled out from other workers and emphasised all that he himself had done "in making the foundations here firm and stable".

The weakness of her last days magnified her sense of neglect. She appears to have been a year without hearing from him and when she received, in December 1914, for the last time a plum pudding, she declared that it was being remembered that gave her a full heart. For his "defection", she said, had taken much zest from life. Thinking he had forgotten her, she no longer cared to get well. Aware that at her death anything connected with her might acquire a kind of magic or even be used as "juju", she had destroyed her personal papers, his letters among them. "I don't want to leave anything of personalities lying about for prying eyes."

The following day, the 25th December, she wrote a Christmas card to Charles's father—as it were a benediction on the family— wishing them every blessing for all the years to come. Three weeks later she was dead.

Like many of her other "laddies", Charles Partridge went off to the war, and saw service in Greece and Italy. His subsequent life is swallowed up in a diffidence so great that even the paper to which he was a long-time contributor was forbidden to publish his obituary. He lived, however, to a good age, in Suffolk, a spruce figure with a military moustache and somewhat old-fashioned tastes, his youthful liking for innovatory gadgets like phonographs and bicycles evidently expended.

We cannot know what he made of the resounding fame of the lonely woman who held him in such warm affection and for ten years made him her confidant. But he did preserve her letters.

17

HOMAGE

In the Mary Slessor Room of the City Museum at Dundee can be seen Mary's diaries for the years 1912 and 1914, written in large ledger books in a fine, well-formed hand that was often shaky with fever.

The brief jottings, once deciphered, are strangely moving, reflecting as they do her daily preoccupations. One feels dragged down by recurrent fever and dysentry, and what sounds at times like starvation. "The workmen make such a hole in my pocket," she wrote. "It is very difficult to get money brought from Calabar and then the people won't take English money when it comes. They use copper wires." One is hardly surprised to find the entry, "Fowls lost. No food but herring and oatmeal", followed by: "Vomited bile all night. Diarrhoea all day."

Nevertheless, she was "On roof all day, head and neck aching, hands broken and bleeding."

The children, like herself, were tough and worked hard:

Market. Tired out. Bush clearing. Jean making corn patch. Maggie and Whitie mudding and carrying sand ... Alice ironing ... mending tattered Bibles and books ...

And how she worried about them! About Maggie who "fell through the rungs of the ladder, and for a time was insensible"; about Mary, now a young mother who, it was rumoured, might be posted to Lagos with her husband—"a mere bairn herself, and an infant in arms and no-one with her. I'm just knocked over ..."

At Use, in the course of one week in February, the entries show, she had the burying of three babies.

In April there were other difficulties:

First thing on sweeping this morning after a sleepless night was to find the white ants in millions in the drawers. God was good to shew me so soon. Very little damage done, but one hour longer and everything would have been destroyed. Had to send scholars home ... many not well.

In the next few days she records a "high fever before prayers" and a night of delirium — "still, am able to be about, teach school and wash a big washing."

The handwriting deteriorates and one is grateful to read that the young Dr. Hitchcock, who had relieved Dr. Robertson at Itu, comes over fairly frequently. Mary first found John Hitchcock a doctor "to whom it is a pleasure to do anything for a sick child", but soon discovered under his mild manners a will to match her own. When, anxious to ensure she had an adequate diet, he sent her over a chicken, and Mary indignantly demanded to know why, he retorted, "Because it could not come by itself." He was determined to prevent her excursions to Ikpe. This led, by the doctor's account, to a "collision".

> . . . I only stopped her by threatening to close all work at Itu and follow her. This was effectual, and since then she has been amenable. She has been really very ill — it is her heart, and I am obliged to see her every day. She has only a native house — the floor is of beaten earth, the walls of clay, the windows are bits of absent wall . . . I am glad she is improving, but she is so frightfully headstrong.

To the young doctor she was an old woman, a "poor soul . . . utterly heroic". But in the course of repeated visits he succumbed to her unfailing fascination and declared her "a statesman". To his mother he wrote:

> . . . Often her wit flashes out and splendid discernment shows itself. She is quite a small woman — fair hair, clear complexion, exceedingly vivacious, an excellent conversationalist.
>
> Tea on the verandah. A big box for a table, boxes for seats. For tablecloth, Jean — wonderful Jean — brings a damask towel. One knife. Water biscuits and some strawberry jam on a plate. At one end of the verandah three or four squealing infants . . . But what a fine woman she is, with a magnificent brain.

Mary thought the world of this newcomer ("I am beginning to love him like a son") but complained, ". . . to the doctor my health is the only thing, but I can't get rest for body while my mind is torn about things. He is vexed and I am vexed at vexing him." That the doctor was often summoned by Jean or Miss Peacock without her knowledge irritated her and she would sabotage his efforts if she could. For even now the threat of being invalided home, away from the people and children she loved, menaced her peace of mind.

Those who appreciated Mary delighted in her company still. Mr. Macgregor speaks of her "quick sympathy . . . immense circle of friends" and of her conversation "rich in allusion, witty, full of keen insight into men and affairs". Yet many stories attest to the difficulty of working with her in these later years. She could be irascible and stubborn and as her reputation grew, so did her power to irritate. Missionaries who had worked as long and under conditions as hard as she held diametrically opposite views. Alexander Cruickshank could not abide her helter-skelter ways. His training of his boys was so intensive they even spoke Efik with an Aberdeen accent. He could see no point in Mary's "mud kirks" that were hardly more than an assemblage of sticks plastered over with clay, nor in schools taught by the semi-literate.

At one meeting of the Mission Council Mary had adopted, as usual, a highly independent line from which nothing would budge her. The men, at lunch together, were remarking how very trying she had been. Her admirer, Dr. Wilkie, tried to excuse her on grounds that she was ill. "Aye", agreed Mr. Cruickshank, laying down his knife and fork with slow deliberation, "and it's been a *lang* illness."

Martha Peacock put herself out of court with Mary by opposing her in Council and relations were severely strained as they travelled back on the launch to Itu. Next day the younger woman walked over to Use in some apprehension. There, on the step of her mud "cottage", sat Mary, poring over the book of Exodus. When she looked up it was to muse aloud, "Puir wee Mosie! He never did reach the promised land!" Then, with an affectionate, shame-faced grin and a squeeze of the other's arm she exclaimed, "Come awa' in, lassie, I'm awfu' glad to see you!"

A visiting Mission secretary faced an uncomfortable evening with his hostess after a disagreement that caused her to stalk from the room, refusing to speak to him further. At supper-time they took their places in silence. But, when grace had been said, he looked up to find the mischievous old lady sticking out her tongue at him like an unrepentant schoolgirl.

Once an arrival who announced himself as the new Vice-Consul got as rejoinder, "I kenna help that, laddie!" But worse was the story told on himself by a latter-day District Commissioner who probably had the misfortune to put in his appearance when Mary's relations with the government were not of the best. Hearing who he was, she surveyed his slight stature and unimpressive bearing with a scornful eye and commented, "The District Commissioner are ye! They *used* to get gentlemen in the government service!"

Given the extreme propriety of many of her generation, her off-handedness in matters of dress caused not merely embarrassment but positive offence. To overlook such behaviour in a woman of her age as kicking off her shoes in sedate shipboard company required a strenuous effort of charity. Mr. Gardiner of Arochuku, when accompanying her on trek, would insist on walking in front to be spared the sight of Mary in her single cotton garment, often damp from the heat or rains and clinging to her skin.

Once, when travelling on the river, he saw a canoe in the shallows which he recognised as Miss Slessor's and ordered his paddlers to steer alongside. As the distance between the two craft diminished he hailed her, realising too late and in considerable consternation that he had interrupted Mary's bath. But the Queen of Okoyong in no way shared his discomfiture. All he heard from the far side of the canoe were some hasty splashings and a voice demanding, "Jeanie, y'baggage, gie us a pin!"

She caused the already overworked Mission doctors much trouble. Anyone else in her condition would have been sent home for treatment. But Dr. Hitchcock, on hearing she was ill, once spent three days tracking her down at Ikpe only to find she had recovered without assistance. There was strong pressure upon her to take her leave. Instead, Mary requested the "box on wheels" she had considered once before and, as her wish had the strength of command in the home Church, a basketwork wheel-chair, with shafts in front for pulling, was despatched by a Glasgow congregation. This "rickshaw" gave her such increased mobility that she put home leave right out of her mind.

But she soon had to admit the need of change. "I'm lame and feeble and foolish; the wrinkles are wonderful—no concertina is so wonderfully folded and convoluted. I'm a wee, wee wifie, verra little buikit—but I grip on well, none the less." She was with difficulty persuaded to accept the pressing invitation of a Miss Cook in Edinburgh to spend a month in the Canary Islands with all expenses paid. But when a mission box full of warm dress material arrived, she felt reassured that God was on the side of a holiday.

Jean went with her, the pair of them shy and strange in the face of such supreme self-indulgence as a rest in the lovely, sub-tropical setting of Grand Canary. The mission ladies had run up suitable dresses, knowing that Mary would otherwise wear not only whatever garments came handy but outlandish combinations of them.

Mary promised faithfully to wear the dresses and, *on the way back*, on shipboard, where she sat at the Captain's table, surprised the other passengers by appearing at breakfast every morning in a new frock, thus keeping her word.

The absence of public engagements had made this short leave more beneficial than many months among her importunate fellow-Scots. But an ordeal awaited her on arrival in Calabar. For Sir Frederick Lugard, making his first official visit there as Governor of the newly united Nigeria, in his sea-going launch *Ivy*, had particularly asked to meet her. She was reluctantly manoeuvred into the limelight to shake the great man's hand. "The worn, shabbily dressed little woman was brought up to Lugard, standing in all his plumed official dignity, and the two kinds of authority confronted each other. Lugard took her hand and said he was proud to do so."[*]

His brother, Edward, wrote in his diary that day:

> Reading her life story—as I recently had occasion to do in drafting a dispatch to the Secretary of State asking for H.M.'s bestowal of some recognition of her great service . . . a great lump rises in one's throat. The long years of *not* quiet but fierce devotion—for they say she is a tornado—unrecognised and without hope of, or desire for, recognition . . .

Two Duke Town doctors put Mary through a stern health examination and passed her, at sixty-four, as fit for many years to come *if* she would only take care of herself. It was a big "if" but she genuinely intended to try: "God wants us to be efficient, and we cannot be so except by living decently and taking care of the wonderful body he has given us." But, as no one came forward to relieve her at Ikpe or Use, she was soon again trying to do the work of several people.

> What ails our big church [she wrote] with all its wealth of young life—aye, and older life too? . . . If the men and women could be found, the lesser gift of money would surely be liberated. It is the living Spirit of God that we need in our midst.

Given that "living Spirit" she was convinced that service in the world would be no problem. For she once said, "*Do*, lassie, *do*? You've not go to *do*, you've just got to *be*, and the doing will follow." She begged the young women at home not to grow up nervous old maids but to gird themselves for battle and keep their hearts young.

> I'm a witness to the perfect joy and satisfaction of a single life—

[*] Margery Perham, *Lugard, The Years of Authority*, Collins, 1960.

with a tail of human tag-rag hanging on. It is rare! It is as exhilarating as an aeroplane or a dirigible or whatever they are that are always trying to get up and are always coming down!

In July 1913 Mary went back to Okoyong for the first time in seven years, invited by Miss Amess to the opening of a new church at Akpap. She took all of her family but the married girls with her so that the people might see what fine people the once abhorred and discarded babies had become. For several days people from surrounding villages swarmed round the mission house to see and touch their old "Ma" once again. Mary held court on the verandah, too excited to go in for meals.

She and Ma Eme, her "dear friend and almost sister", plunged into reminiscences of the bad old days when the secret link between them had saved so many lives. Hundreds attended service in the not-quite-completed church, to hear Mary speak, but Ma Eme was not among them, for she had never embraced Christianity. "And yet", wrote Mary, "God cannot forget all she was to me, and all she helped me to do in those dark and bloody days."

In July 1913 Mary was bidden to Calabar to receive from the Provincial Commissioner the honour for which Lugard had recommended her. She was elected Honorary Associate in the Order of St. John of Jerusalem, an order dedicated to the relief of the sick and suffering.

Mary had hoped to escape a public presentation of the badge, a Maltese cross of white enamel (now in the Dundee Museum) but, finding it impossible to do so, accepted it as a tribute to Christian Missions at large and declared simply, "If I have done anything in my life it has been easy because the Master has gone before."

A series of social events had been planned in Mary's honour and congratulatory telegrams, letters and flowers poured in upon her. In spite of her embarrassment at being so singled out, Mary found much to enjoy in reunions with old friends and contact with the rising generation of boys and girls at the Hope Waddell Institute. But as soon as the government launch had set her down once more at Itu, she made tracks as quickly as she could for Ikpe. "I shall never look the world in the face again until all this blarney and publicity is over . . . I feel so glad that I can hide here quietly where no-one knows about newspapers and *Records* and do my small portion of work out of sight."

The road under construction from Ikot Ekpene stopped five miles short of Ikpe at Odoro Ikpe, where there was a government Rest

House, and Mary was privileged to ask Mr. Brooks, the District
Commissioner, for his car to take her thus far and save her the long
canoe journey. But she did not often ask for it ". . . I may not keep
the driver for fear he gets into trouble—he is Mary's husband, so
my own son—!" Once at Ikpe itself she was off all lines of com-
munication—more completely cut off than the Arctic explorer is
today—and was without visitors, mail or supplies for weeks on end.
Once she went seven weeks "without a scrap of paper" from the
outside world and was reduced to reading the newspapers that lined
her boxes until she had completely memorised the travel advertise-
ments, and said she could name the hotels in any town in Europe.

Her living conditions were as rough as in her first years at Okoyong, and the conservatism of the people was as deep. Everywhere
she was met with the cry, "You will be letting twins and twin-
mothers into our midst to kill us." To which Mary would reply, let
them show her the village that was any the worse for her coming.

The heart-breaking campaign to get twins accepted went on, but
it was now the general policy to leave them in their homes. Therefore, when a case arose in which the father of twins was narrowly
prevented from killing the surviving twin and its mother and tossing them into a swamp, Mary installed Jean in their home to guard
them. But, while Jean was at church, the mother lamed and
poisoned the baby, who was then removed to the mission house and
nursed back to health. At two and a half months he was a fine and
healthy baby and his parents reclaimed him. But within a few days
the child was dead—the depressing end, for Jean, of "ten weeks'
toil by day and night".

Mary covered a lot of ground in her "rickshaw . . . with six lads
to push and pull and carry the car through". The remarkable Jean
seems to have filled in everywhere at once. Now the "sons-in-law",
David the driver, and Akpan, a dedicated layman, played their part.
Mary gives a glimpse of these intricate family dispositions in a letter
from Use in January 1914:

I was troubled as to how I was to get lunch ready for next
morning, as we had to be [at the opening of the new Use church]
early, and I had left Janie at Ikot Ekpene with Mary and her new
baby, and Annie had to provide hospitality for her husband's
people in her own home. But just at the darkening came Mary,
her two children, Jean and Whitie, and all my anxieties fled. I
knew the chicken would be caught, killed, cooked, and all ready
without my intervention. David was bringing in the car to within

five miles for an officer, and he got the whole bunch brought on that length, then a roadman gave them an extra carrier for the baby, and all got here well. The baby only a fortnight old. Oh, hadn't we a great night! We did not turn in till ten o'clock, and that means midnight here. They stayed for nearly a week with us, and the church people were so pleased. David got away and ran across on his cycle on the Sabbath, so if only Dan and Asuquo had been here we should have been an unbroken family.

A month later she was camping in the government Rest House at Odoro Ikpe, high on an escarpment.

For the last six days we have been living the simple life, and are gypsying by the roadside in a mud house without doors and innocent of windows other than holes in the wall, and with Miss Peacock's camp bed on loan and my wheel-chair as our kit and furniture, a pail from the prison, and a cooking pot and plate from the barracks being our kitchen and bedroom outfit . . . The wardrobe is being washed at the spring in the town, and dried on the fence here, piece by piece, and only the sugar and bread have run out . . .

On Ash Wednesday, her diary records, she was not yet dressed in the morning when the chiefs came to ask if she would "sit down with them in truth", i.e. settle amongst them. "If so, let me walk with them to see where I'd choose to put my house. Needless to add, I rose and went, in my nightdress, which is the same as evening dress to them, and after encompassing the hill top several times, we fixed on a clear bit between the town and the Rest House on the brow of the hill . . ."

Here began Mary's last building operation, a mud house of six tiny rooms on two floors, with a sort of hen-ladder to get in upstairs. Mary almost had it built round her, for if she left the scene for long the building stopped.

Only an infinite restlessness of spirit could have driven her on to this last move and a fresh period of directing an untrained, unreliable labour force in the blistering sun. Even what she called her "new accession of strength" could scarcely sustain three mission stations with their attendant classes, services and domestic problems. In none can she have done much more than awaken the desire of the people to learn. But one senses that in her role as the "feet of the Church" she had a mystical conviction that if she so much as walked — or was carried — over new ground, she had taken it for Christ.

In August she was spending her days in the house with the workmen still finishing and the mud not dry enough to allow for sleeping there. Down below, as she sat in her upper room letting her thoughts run onto paper for Miss Amess at Akpap, Alice was beating the sand floor. "The rain is getting obstreperous . . . there is much sneezing among the mudders", she wrote. Inevitable delays in the building operation had prevented her getting back to "long suffering — and, I fear, grumbling — Use".

News of the outbreak of war had reached her and she was deeply troubled, both for her homeland and for the many young men she knew and loved. She also dreaded what might happen to areas under British influence overseas, for when Germany had taken control of the Cameroons many British missionaries had been turned out.

Her mind ranged nervously over a multitude of subjects, returning always to the better use of manpower in their own mission. She felt women should be released from the staff in Calabar to "flit in here or here away, among the Ibibio further in till we hem them round the Head of the Enyong Creek . . . *Women can do the spade work best.*" But she was aware that these strictures would not be much heeded and reminded herself: "O dear Miss Slessor you are on the warpath again, and God does not work that way, and it is quite possible that other people may be right — and you not far from wrong!"

She had a severe attack of fever in that lonely place, complicated by dysentery and vomiting. The entries in her diary dwindled to five or six words: "Only able for short services" . . . "Dan keeping school" . . . "Fastened to the house."

On the 24th September her condition was grave and the entry goes: "Boys came for me, lifted me in camp bed, and took me to Ikpe — so tenderly. Four fowls smothered to death on the road. Boy took my cat and lost it in the bush." In the morning they made her as comfortable as they could in a canoe and paddled her down to Itu. The doctor was called and went with them to Use, thinking it unlikely she would live till morning.

She rallied, but in the next few weeks thought several times that death was near and destroyed all her personal papers. She had dreaded dying right out in the bush where, since she was considered to be a person of extraordinary powers, her skull, or some other part of her body, might be taken in the expectation that it would make powerful "medicine".

When Dan returned from school for the Christmas recess he burst into tears at her wasted appearance. But, though life was slipping away, Mary was where she wanted to be, among her adopted people, surrounded by her "children" and "grandchildren". She could still be carried to church to lead the services and as late as the 2nd January could write: "Annie's wee girlie is the sweetest pet, and imitates everything and everybody. She runs about in church, and will point to me during the service and call to me, yet I *can't* say, don't bring her. There should be room in our Father's House even for the babies."

In the second week of January she collapsed for the last time, and suffered on, semi-conscious, for several days. She was closely tended by Dr. Robertson, the two friends from Ikot Obong, and her five girls, who knew better than most the signs of impending death. At times she was heard to pray in the Efik that came so naturally to her, "O Abasi, sana mi yok" (O God, release me). She died quietly just before dawn on the morning of Wednesday, the 13th January, 1915.

18

GREATNESS PASSING

THE FUNERAL IN Calabar was as splendid as government pomp
and missionary eloquence could make it. Flags were lowered to half-
mast, schools and offices closed, as people thronged to pay last
respects to one who, in the thirty-eight years since she had first
landed in Duke Town, had become *Eka kpukpru owo*, "Everybody's mother". Police lined the roads from the wharf to Mission
Hill, along which the mahogany coffin was borne, and school-
children craned to see (in the phrase of Professor Eyo Ita, who was
one of them) "greatness passing by".

Mary Slessor was buried in the cemetery overlooking the har-
bour, beside her old friends, the Andersons, and near to where, very
soon, her dear, vexing Dr. Hitchcock would lie. Tribute upon
tribute was heaped upon her.

But when it was all over some wondered what had become of the
tough, humorous little Scotswoman they remembered. One of the
carpenters who had roughed it with her in the bush remarked,
"That was a fine service, but it wasn't the Miss Slessor *I* knew."
And, as the pious legend of her life began to gather strength, there
were those who objected, "She was nae sae holy!"

But to the Africans "holiness" was beside the point. It was her
wholehearted identification with them and their needs that secured
her a lasting place in the hearts of Efik, Okoyong, Aro and Ibibio.

When her young friend Mrs. Arnot went to Arochuku in 1916 to
found the Mary Slessor Memorial Home for Girls, the people said,
"We knew you would come. Ma said she would send someone."

Twenty years later, the Rev. R. M. Macdonald of the great Itu
Leper Colony that was an offshoot of the Mary Slessor Hospital,
was giving a magic lantern show at Ikpe Ikot Nkun. He ended with
a picture of Mary herself. As the projector switched off and the well-
known face faded, apparently absorbed into the white sheet that had
served as a screen, an old chief begged to be allowed to have the
cloth because, he said, his fine old face crinkling into smiles, "I
liked dat woman too much!"

Fifty years after her death Mary Slessor's was still a name to conjure with, and many of the people in the districts where she had lived joined in paying homage to her memory. She would have smiled to see her adventures, now part of the local folk-lore, re-enacted in the inimitable mime of an African "play" — a well-dressed, cheerful troupe of women paddling an imaginary canoe and flailing a non-existent hippopotamus for the benefit of a new generation of children and a film-making unit from Britain.

The Civil War two years later ravaged the country more cruelly than the worst depredations of the slave trade. The hospital at Itu, the naming of which threw Mary Slessor into such transports of modest confusion, lay bombed and in ruins. "Dear old Calabar" was the scene of atrocities. Three of the "grandchildren", Dan's daughters, were taken prisoner. The people who in her day began to conceive of themselves as a nation were reverting to the narrow tribalism of a century before.

In this holocaust, schools, churches and hospitals are destroyed. Thousands have died of starvation. What seemed to be a success story has been recast as rank tragedy. Who knows whether in this extremity there may not come a regression to the "old fashions", none of which was wholly dead, so that twin murder, trial by esere bean and human sacrifice once more become respectable.

Yet, wherever along the lower reaches of the Cross River, and particularly the Enyong Creek, an African woman earns her own living; wherever a mother of twins rears her children and her husband stands loyally by her; wherever parties to a quarrel seek the mediation of the courts instead of leaping for their matchets, something endures of the spirit of a slight, red-haired woman who in the midst of this region was whirlwind, earthquake, fire, and still small voice.

SOURCES

MOST OF THE known facts about Mary Slessor are contained in *Mary Slessor of Calabar, Pioneer Missionary*, by W. P. Livingstone (1915) and in his book for young people, *The White Queen of Okoyong* (1916) on which numerous other books are based. Much is to be learned from the missionary magazines which printed her reports and excerpts from her private correspondence, the *Women's Missionary Magazine* and the *Missionary Record* of the United Free Church of Scotland. The Dundee Public Library, City Museum and Wishart Memorial Church all have letters and other source material. The National Library of Scotland preserves Mission Records.

The following were invaluable for background material:

Ajayi, J. F. A. *Christian Missions in Nigeria 1841–1891, The Making of a New Elite*, London, 1965.

Campbell, Olwen, *Mary Kingsley, A Victorian in the Jungle*, London, 1957.

Cole, G. D. H. and Postgate, Raymond, *The Common People*, London, 1938.

Crowder, Michael, *The Story of Nigeria*, London, 1962.

Dike, K. Onwuka, *Trade and Politics in the Niger Delta 1830–1885*, London, 1956.

Forde, Daryll, *Efik Traders of Old Calabar*, London, 1956.

Forde, Daryll, and Jones, G. I., *The Ibo and Ibibio-speaking Peoples of South-eastern Nigeria*, London, 1950.

Goldie, Hugh, *Calabar and its Mission*, Edinburgh, 1890.

Howard, Cecil, *Mary Kingsley*, London, 1957.

Hogg, Jessie, *The Story of the Calabar Mission*, Edinburgh, 1902.

Johnston, Sir Harry, *The Story of My Life*, London, 1923.

Kingsley, Mary, *Travels in West Africa*, London, 1897.

　West African Studies, London, 1899.

Livingstone, W. P., *Dr. Hitchcock of Uburu*, Edinburgh, 1920.

Luke, James, *Pioneering in Mary Slessor Country*, London, 1929.

Macdonald, Dr. A. B., *In His Name*, London, 1964.

McFarlan, Donald, *Calabar*, London, 1946.

Marwick, W., *William and Louisa Anderson*, Edinburgh, 1897.

Meek, C. K., *Law and Authority in a Nigerian Tribe*, London, 1937.

Parrinder, G., *African Traditional Religion*, London, 1954.
    Witchcraft, London, 1958.

Perham, Margery, *Lugard, The Years of Authority*, London, 1960.

Talbot, D. Amaury, *Woman's Mysteries of a Primitive People*, London, 1915.

Thorp, Ellen, *Ladder of Bones*, London, 1956.

Waddell, Hope, *Twenty-nine Years in the West Indies and Central Africa*, London, 1863.

Whitford, John, *Trading Life in West and Central Africa*, Liverpool, 1877.

On Scotland:

Miller, T. Y., *Dundee Past and Present*, Dundee, 1909.

Dundee Advertiser Centenary Memoir, Dundee, 1901.

Ferguson, Thomas, *Scottish Social Welfare*, Edinburgh, 1958.

Holmes, E. M., *History of Education in Scotland*, London, 1942.

Mackie, R. L., *Short History of Scottish Education*, Edinburgh, 1962.

INDEX